Is every knot
without a name.

THE COMPLETE BOOK OF

Knots

Geoffrey Budworth

The Lyons Press

The Complete Book of Knots
Geoffrey Budworth

First published in 1997 by Hamlyn
an imprint of Octopus Publishing Group Ltd
2-4 Heron Quays, Docklands, London E14 4JP

10 9 8 7 6 5 4 3
Library of Congress Cataloging-in-Publication data is
available on file.

ISBN 1-55821-632-4

Publishing Director Laura Bamford

Executive Editor Simon Tuite
Project Editor Katie Cowan
Editors Tracey Beresford and Caroline Bingham

Art Director Keith Martin
Executive Art Editor Mark Stevens
Design Town Group Consultancy Limited
Illustration Line and Line
Photography Gary Latham

Production Mark Walker

The publishers have made every effort to ensure that all
instructions given in this book are accurate and safe, but
they cannot accept liability for any resulting injury, damage
or loss to either person or property whether direct or
consequential and howsoever arising. The author and
publishers will be grateful for any information which will
assist them in keeping future editions up to date.

Typeset in Adobe Myriad, Monotype Walbaum and
Monotype Grotesque

Produced by Toppan Printing Co Ltd
Printed in China

contents

the knots

DIRECTORY OF KNOTS

The solid circle shows the best or most popular use of each knot; the open circles show the other areas in which that knot also has applications.

KNOT	PAGE	⛵	🔄	⛰	⛱	🏠	DESCRIPTION
Ashley's stopper knot	32	●	○	○	○	○	Bulky stopper knot for all occasions
Monkey's fist	33	●	○				Classic knot for throwing lines
Lapp knot	34	●	○			○	Quick-release waist attachment, etc.
Bowline	36	●	○		○	○	General purpose, single fixed loop
Bowline in the bight	38	●	○	○	○	○	Fixed twin loops tied without access to ends
Fisherman's knot	39	●	○			○	Compact bend for cord or rope
Sheet bend	40	●	○			○	Traditional join for lines of somewhat different size
Seizing bend	42	●	○				Extra secure for very dissimilar lines
Carrick bend	43	●	○		○		Strong join for large hawsers or cables
Zeppelin bend	44	●	○				Strong undo-able bend for the heaviest shock loads
Knute hitch	45	●	○	○	○	○	Simple lanyard or halyard attachment
Mooring hitch	46	●	○				Versatile, slide-&-jam, quick-release mooring hitch
Killick hitch	47	●	○				Pulling or towing holdfast, or anchorage
Clove hitch	48	●	○		○	○	Versatile mooring hitch, etc.
Rolling hitch	49	●	○			○	Resists a lengthwise pull
Snuggle hitch	50	●	○				Strong and secure hitch to rail or post
Buntline hitch	51	●	○	○	○	○	Attaches a line securely to a ring eye, etc
Round turn & two half-hitches	52	●	○			○	Useful mooring hitch, etc.
Anchor bend	53	●					Secures wet lines to rings, etc.
Lighterman's hitch	54	●	○				Towing or mooring hitch, guy-line attachment
Heaving line knot	58	○	●	○			Adds weight to a thrown heaving line
Boa knot	60		●			○	Most robust binding knot
Bowstring knot and loop	62		●				Tensions cord at its point of attachment
Manharness knot	63		●				Shoulder loop for hauling a load
Scaffold knot	64	○	●			○	Versatile adjustable loop
Midshipman's hitch	65		●				Semi-permanent hitch to rail or spar
Handcuff knot	66		●				Twin adjustable loop for odd tasks
Tarbuck knot	67		●	○			General purpose slide-&-jam knot
Vice versa	68		●				Interwoven bend for slippery thongs, etc.
Icicle hitch	70	○	●			○	Extraordinary hitch for a lengthwise pull
Pile hitch	72		●			○	Versatile knot for end or bight attachment to post
Highwayman's hitch	73	○	●			○	Quick release halter or mooring hitch
Pole hitch	74	○	●			○	Lashing for long poles, etc.
Half-hitching	75	○	●			○	Parcelling
Marline hitching	76	○	●			○	Parcelling
Chain stitch lashing	77	○	●			○	Secure yet quick-release lashing for awkward bundles
Trucker's hitch	78		●			○	Tensions load lashings, etc.
Diamond hitch	79		●				Lashing for loads carried by animal or luggage rack
Jug, jar or bottle sling	80	○	●	○	○	○	Twin carrying handles for liquid containers
Frost knot	84			●			Makes tape or webbing stirrups (étriers)
Alpine butterfly	86			●			Attaches the middle climber to a rope

<6>

KNOT	PAGE	⛵	➰	⛰	🐐	🏠	DESCRIPTION
Figure eight loops	88		○	●		○	Stopper knot for the end of rope or cord
Triple bowline & variation	92		○	●			Creates a sit sling, chest sling or full harness
Trident loop	94			●			Tie-in alternative to the figure of eight loop
Adjustable loop and bend	95		○	●			Slide and grip shock-absorbing bend
Flemish bend	96		○	●			Joins ropes
Overhand shortening	97			●			Makes leg loops in tape (webbing)
Double & triple fisherman's knot	98			●			Bulkier, but stronger version of the fisherman's knot
Tape knot	100		○	●			Sole knot recommended for tying tape
Munter friction hitch	102			●			Energy absorbing belay
Prusik knot	104			●			Classic slide and grip knot
Bachman knot	106			●			Sliding friction knot
Klemheist knot	107			●			Prusiking friction knot
Extended French Prusik knot	108			●			Innovative Prusik knot for tape
Palomar knot	112				●		Attaches most lines to hooks, lures, swivels or arbors
Jansik special	113				●		Strong knot for attaching hooks, lures or swivels
Angler's loop knot	114	○	○		●	○	Fixed loop to attach to just about anything
Blood loop dropper knot	116				●		Strong start to a paternoster system
Surgeon's loop	117		○		●		Attaches lures, hooks, swivels
Arbor knot	118				●		Attaches line to reel spool
Bimini twist	119		○		●		Strongest loop for big-game fishing
Grinner knot	120				●		Joins lines
Blood knot	122				●		Joins monofilaments of almost similar sizes
Linfit knot	124	○	○		●	○	Joins stiff and springy lines
Albright knot	125				●		Joins dissimilar-sized monofilaments
Spade end knot	126	○	○		●		Ties monofilament to spade-ended hooks
Snelling	127				●		Mainly for sea fishing hooks and lures
Half-blood knot	128				●		Attaches hooks, lures and swivels
Turle knot	129				●		For a straight pull on up- or downturned eyes
True lover's knot	130	○	○		●	○	Small fixed knot for lures
Offshore knot	131				●		Swivel or hook attachment
Reef knot (square knot)	134	○	○			●	Ties off parcels, bandages and such like
Constrictor knot	136	○	○	○	○	●	Best binding knots for most occasions
Square knot	140	○	○	○	○	●	Decorative knot for a scarf, lanyard, etc.
Strangle knot	142	○	○			●	Useful bag knot, etc.
Pedigree cow hitch	143	○	○			●	Quick, simple hitch to post or rail
Cow hitch variation	144	○	○			●	Attachment to post or rail
Halter hitch	145		○			●	Tethers animals of all kinds
Cat's paw	146	○	○		○	●	Secure attachment to hook or rail
Parcel ties	147					●	String knots
Fireman's chair knot	148	○	○			●	Emergency rescue knot
Instant knot trick	150					●	Trick knot
Impossible knot trick	151					●	Trick knot
Knots galore trick	152					●	Trick knot
Threading-the-needle trick	153					●	Trick knot
Finger-trap trick	154					●	Trick knot

<7>

ACKNOWLEDGEMENTS

Because knot tying is often a solitary pursuit I tend to say I am self-taught but that is not strictly true. Over more than 45 years I have absorbed much of what is in the hundreds of knot books I now own and so must gratefully acknowledge their writers and illustrators. In the 1960s and 70s I had a friend and knot-tying mentor, the late James Nicoll, who extended my capabilities. Following the foundation in 1982 of the International Guild of Knot Tyers, I was shown all kinds of knotlore by my accomplished IGKT colleagues.

I am especially indebted to the following Guild members, whose expertise has contributed directly or indirectly to the contents of this book: Charles Warner (Australia); Robert Chisnall (Canada); Peter van de Griend (Faroe Islands); Robert Pont (France); Sten Johansson and Frank Rosenow (Sweden); Harry Asher, Percy W. Blandford, Lester Copestake, Stuart Grainger, Colin Grundy, Desmond Mandeville, Owen K. Nuttall, John Smith, Ettrick W. Thomson and Nola Trower (UK); Barbara Merry, Dan R. Lehman, Max Nicholls, Mike Storch, Brion Toss and Robert M. Wolfe (USA). Finally, I should like to thank Peter Collingwood for permission to include his remarkable discovery, the boa knot; also Captain Simon Waite and The Maritime Trust at

<8>

Greenwich for their generous permission to use the resources of the historic clipper ship **Cutty Sark.**

I duly acknowledge the generous permission of literary agents A.P. Watt Ltd. on behalf of Cystal Hale and Jocelyn Herbert to include in this publication two extracts from the Bowline, a poem by the late A.P. (Sir Alan) Herbert.

The photographer would like to thank all at Master Rope Makers, The Historic Dockyard, Chatham, Kent , and the fishermen of Hastings, England. Thanks also to Geoff Budworth for his magnificent expertise, kind advice and for supplying specific knots.

*The timber hitch,
the reef knot, the sheet and
fishermen's bends,*

*The clove, the sweet and
simple hitch on which so much
depends,*

*Have each a special duty
which they do perfectly
discharge*

*(Much more than you can say
of men and matters
by and large).*

Sir Alan P. Herbert, 1890-1971

<9>

introduction

KNOTLORE

Knots pre-date written history; by the time humankind's story began to be recorded, rope and cordage, together with the knots then used to make them work, were already established. In 1923 an ancient piece of fishing net found preserved in a peat bog at Antrea, in pre-war Finland, was scientifically dated at 7,200 BC. This makes the knots in it – which were the same as some used today – the oldest found so far. There is circumstantial evidence that cave dwellers knew the simple overhand knot, the overhand noose, granny and reef knots, the weaver's knot or sheet bend, and there are records to prove that the Ancient Greeks, Romans and Egyptians used complex knots for everything from bridge building to surgery and sorcery.

Some knots seem to have been universal, no doubt arising spontaneously wherever someone sat down to discover, by trial and error, what could be done with a piece of cord. Knowledge of others must have been spread via conquest and trade routes. Bruce Grant, author of the **Encyclopedia of Rawhide and Leather Braiding**, has commented that it may be possible to trace the entire course of Spanish civilization through the history of the Spanish woven knot, a version of the Turk's head long used by sailors.

Knots, bends and hitches are generally assumed to have been the speciality of deep-water sailormen who crewed square-rigged ships, perhaps because the earliest books to feature knots were often eighteenth and nineteenth century seamanship manuals. This link has been reinforced by all of the nostalgic literature that followed. In his book (**A Gypsy of the Horn**) published in 1924, Rex Clements writes of 'Working cunning knots and splices dear to the old-time sailor's heart'. In fact, at least as much ropework went on ashore as afloat, and in past centuries there have been anglers' knots, builders' knots, farmers' knots, gunners' knots, millers' knots, packers' knots, steeplejacks' knots, waggoners' knots and weavers' knots, as well as watermen's knots. Cowboys tied knots and braids every bit as complicated as those done by seamen. Today, anglers and fishermen, cavers and climbers have taken over from sailors in their preoccupation with efficient and effective knots, inventing and naming many new ones.

Knots fall into categories but their family relationships can be mixed and muddled, and are

<12>

A few knots are nameless, but a lot have, over decades or centuries, acquired more than one. The fisherman's knot, for example, can still be found in print as the angler's knot, English knot, Englishman's knot, halibut knot, true lover's knot, water knot and waterman's knot. The double fisherman's knot is also the angler's grapevine or grinner knot, so the triple fisherman's knot (with peculiar arithmetic) is a double grapevine or grinner. Desmond Mandeville, a founder member of the International Guild of Knot Tyers, put it aptly in a poem printed in the Guild's journal **Knotting Matters**:

> *A nameless knot's a foolish thing –*
> *Merely a muddle in a piece of string!*
> *In Geoffrey's Rag,* it makes me rage*
> *To see a squiggle on the page*
> *Without a name. I care no cuss*
> *For your fine Knots Anonymous –*
> *Since any bend that's worth a try*
> *Should have a name, like you or I.*
> *A waste of time, a Knotman's shame*
> *Is every knot without a name.*
> *(Yet worse than those that haven't any,*
> *Some knots there be that have too many.)*

So welcome to the esoteric and often illogical – but always useful and sometimes beautiful – art, craft and science of knots.

* A reference to **Knotting Matters**, of which I was then the editor.

not always obvious until you are introduced to them. Individual knot names are not always helpful either. The fisherman's knot is actually a bend, while the fisherman's bend is a hitch. Tie a knot a different way, for another purpose, and it may be re-named; so the sheet bend tied in yarns becomes the weaver's knot, while the anglers' version of the strangle knot has in recent years resurfaced as the Vare knot.

<13>

TERMS, TIPS AND TECHNIQUES

ROPES AND LINES

Pre-metric knot books refer to rope size by circumference in inches, so a $1^1/_2$-in rope was actually less than $^1/_2$-in thick. Today all cordage is known by its diameter in centimetres (or millimetres), converting the same rope to 12-mm. Rope is traditionally anything over 1-in circumference (10-mm diameter). Ropes for special purposes are referred to as lines (bowline, stern line, tow line, clothes-line). Smaller stuff, as it is informally called, is cordage or (if thinner still) string or twine.

Fibres

Yarns

Strand

1

A three-strand rope (fig. 1) spirals clockwise, as it goes away from you, the strands having a lay that is right-handed. Craftworkers prefer the term Z-laid. Sailors call such a rope a hawser and so it is hawser-laid. The individual strands are twisted left-handed (S-laid) and the yarns of each strand were first spun right-handed. All of this counteracting tension and friction gives rope its form and strength. Laid rope may have more than three strands, which makes it more flexible (although no stronger), but it then has a hollow core, which must be filled with a heart of yarns. Hearts may be laid, unlaid or braided.

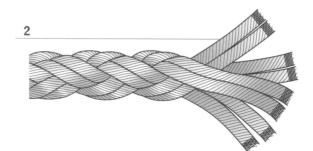

2

Rope is rarely left-handed, except when three hawsers are laid up to make a ship's mooring cable. Cable-laid ropes inevitably have nine strands and consequently must be S-laid. Another way to make giant ropes – say for supertankers – is to plait them with four pairs of strands (fig. 2).

Braided rope (figs 3-5) consists of a sheath – generally of 16 strands – containing a heart (core). Cores may be parallel fibres or monofilaments, or twisted, or plaited. In this last instance, the construction is commonly known as braid-on-braid. Kernmantel (literally, core-sheath) climbing ropes are an example. In such braid-on-braid constructions, both sheath and core may contribute to rope strength. Alternatively, the core could be chosen for one property (e.g., strength or elasticity) and the sheath for another (e.g., resistance to abrasion). A more recent development is to enclose a braided core in its own thin sheath (fig. 6).

Rope, cord, string and twines were once all made from the shredded and combed fibres of plant stems, stalks and leaves. Cotton, coir, sisal, manilla and hemp were the renewable and eco-friendly crops from which vegetable-fibre ropes were made. These natural-fibre ropes had character – conjured up by the smell of tarred marline on working boats, or of soft white cotton aboard smart yachts. But they could be hard on the hands and all the cordage was, by today's standards, weak. Strength only came with cumbersome circumferences. Natural-fibre rope was somewhat stronger when wet (as are synthetics) but then it tended to rot.

Natural-fibre ropes have been replaced almost entirely by modern synthetics. Nylon is marketed under trade names such as Polyamid, Bri-nylon and Enkalon. Polyester appears as Terylene, Dacron, Tergal and Fortrel. The expensive organic polymer aramid is sold as Kevlar. Then there is cheaper polypropylene. Newer products include Dyneema, Spectra and Admiral 2000. A competent supplier will sort out what you need, but basically nylon stretches and so is suitable for anchor warps

<14>

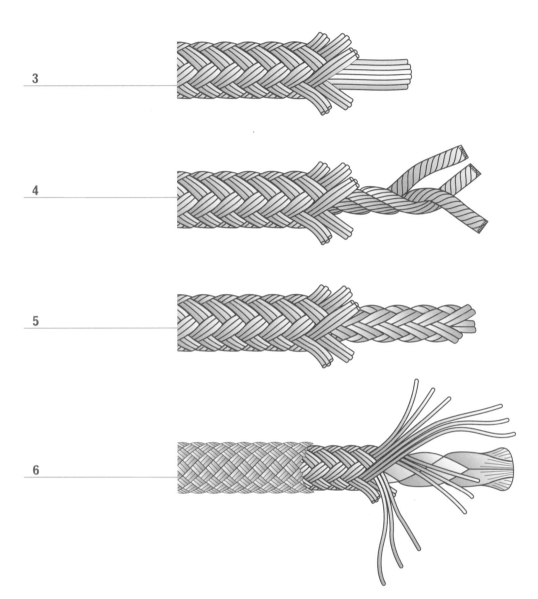

3

4

5

6

or tow lines where some give is crucial, whereas Terylene does not and is used for standing rigging and in any other case where stretch is unwanted. Kevlar has a remarkable strength-to-weight ratio and can replace wire rigging, but it can be easily damaged by abrasion and must be sheathed in tough polyester. Weaker, lighter cordage (e.g. polypropylene) may float and make a useful heaving line. Man-made cordage comes in many colours, so it is now usual to colour code yacht halyards and sheets, or merely to follow fashion in rigging a sail-board or canoe.

The problem with man-made fibre ropes, spun from monofilaments, is that they are smooth and slippery, with less grip, and trusted knots may perform badly in them. The usual advice is to add a half-hitch or two for extra security; the long-term answer may be to come up with more suitable knots. Some manufacturers chop their long monofilaments into shorter staple lengths, which re-creates the hairy surface texture of rope originally made from leaves and stalks and roots of plants.

<15>

STRENGTH AND SECURITY

Strength and security are different characteristics in a knot. Relative knot strength – or efficiency – is the breaking strength of a knotted rope, compared with the same rope unknotted. The overhand knot, for example, has a strength of about 45%; in other words, it more than halves the breaking strength of any line in which it is allowed to remain, so it should not be used for anything vital. A steady pull is not the same as putting a shock loading on a knotted rope (e.g., when a climber falls and is brought up short). Then the momentum equals the mass multiplied by its speed and direction. To withstand such stresses and strains, the rope should be tied with one or other of the slide-and-grip friction knots, which are designed to absorb energy while safeguarding knot and line.

Knots that unintentionally slip or capsize rather than breaking the rope (or before they can break it) are insecure ones. Knots may be strong and secure, or strong but liable to spill if jerked about. Some are secure but weak. A knot cannot be both weak and insecure since, if it comes apart easily, its strength will never be tested.

KNOTS, BENDS AND HITCHES

A knot is the generic name for any loop or entanglement of flexible material, created either intentionally or accidentally, by a tucked end or bight. The word also has a very precise meaning: a knot, as distinct from a bend or hitch (see below), secures two ends of the same material, e.g., a bandage, parcel string or shoelace. In addition, a knot is anything (including a bend or hitch) tied in small stuff – thus all anglers' knots are by definition merely knots, irrespective of form or function.

A bend is a knot that joins two separate ropes or other bits of cordage together.

A hitch attaches a line to a rail, post, ring or perhaps to another rope (or even onto itself).

There is often more than one way to tie complex knots and knot enthusiasts bore and bewilder if they insist on showing them all. This book illustrates one quick and easy way to learn and use each knot, only showing alternative methods where these are needed to cope with different circumstances.

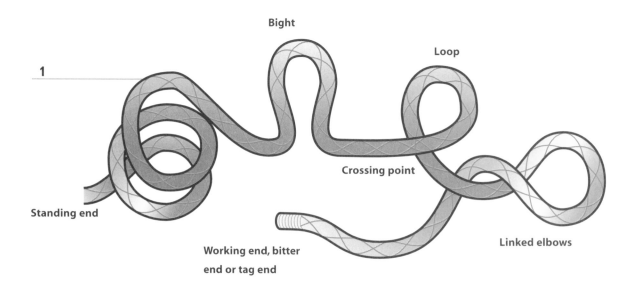

Bight

Loop

1

Crossing point

Standing end

Working end, bitter end or tag end

Linked elbows

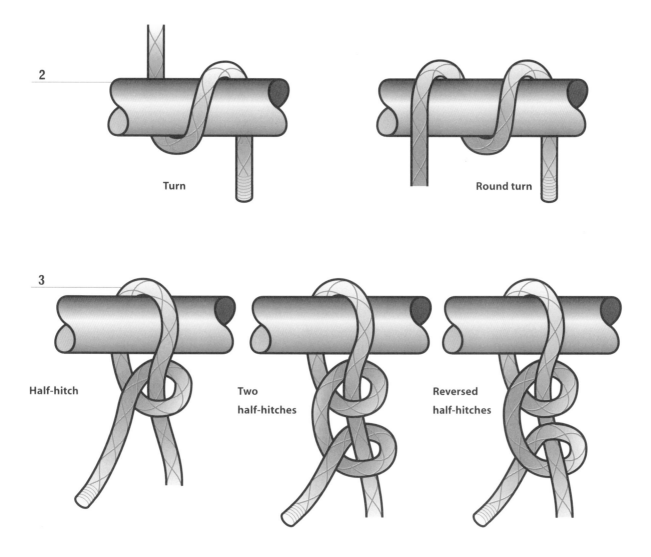

OTHER USEFUL TERMS

The end of a line used to tie knots is referred to as the working end or (by anglers) the tag end or (if it is being pulled out of your hand) the bitter end (fig. 1). The other is the standing end. In-between is the standing part. When this portion of the line is doubled it is called a bight, until it is crossed over itself and becomes a loop, maybe with an elbow.

Wrapping a rope around a post or rail, to take the strain of a moving boat or a heavy load, is called 'taking a turn', but bringing the working end around an extra half a turn, prior to making fast, creates a round turn (fig. 2).

A simple knot with something through it is a half-hitch (fig. 3). Finish off a round turn with two half-hitches rather than two reversed half-hitches.

<17>

ENDS

Overhand knot

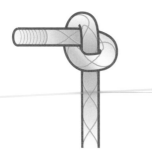

undone than an overhand knot, and with one it may be slightly stronger (45-50%). Do not leave it flat but pull the standing part so that the working end is pulled over and trapped beneath the bight. Although bulkier than the overhand knot, it does not have a larger diameter (contrary to what many knot enthusiasts will tell you). It will pull out of the same size hole as the overhand knot. If you need to use something bigger, choose Ashley's stopper knot (see p. 32).

1

STOPPER KNOTS

String and cord are not cheap so, to minimize waste from fraying, you may tie an overhand knot (fig. 1) in the end. The overhand knot needs no explanation – we can all do it – except to reiterate that it reduces the breaking strength of rope or cordage to a mere 45% of the unknotted line. If the working end is not pulled completely through, leaving a draw-loop (see below), a somewhat stronger (45-50%) stopper knot is made (fig. 2), which can be used to restring musical instruments. To secure something bulkier, tie an overhand knot in the bight (fig. 3).

To prevent jib leads, main halyards, flag halyards, etc., coming unreeved from blocks, fairleads or other slots or holes, use a figure eight knot (figs 4-5). This knot appears to have been named by Darcy Lever in his book **Sheet Anchor** (1908). With or without a draw-loop, it is more easily

Overhand knot with draw-loop

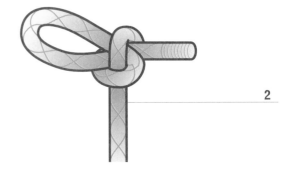

2

<18>

Figure eight knot with draw-loop

3

5

Figure eight knot

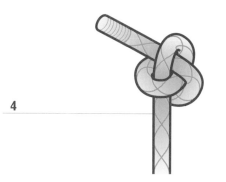

4

DRAW-LOOPS

When the working end is not pulled completely through the knot, a draw-loop is created. Tug on that end and it acts as a quick-release to undo the knot. Mooring and tethering hitches are obvious examples of draw-loops. The highwayman's hitch (see p. 73), for instance, is just one draw-loop after another. Many other knots may be improved in this way. Some, such as the common bowline, may actually be strengthened by the extra rope part within the body of the knot. Such knots are also less likely to jam. So, unless you want a semi-permanent knot, draw-loops should be used wherever possible. Note that if you treat both working ends of a reef knot (see p. 134) as draw-loops, you will end up with the familiar double reef bow used to tie shoelaces.

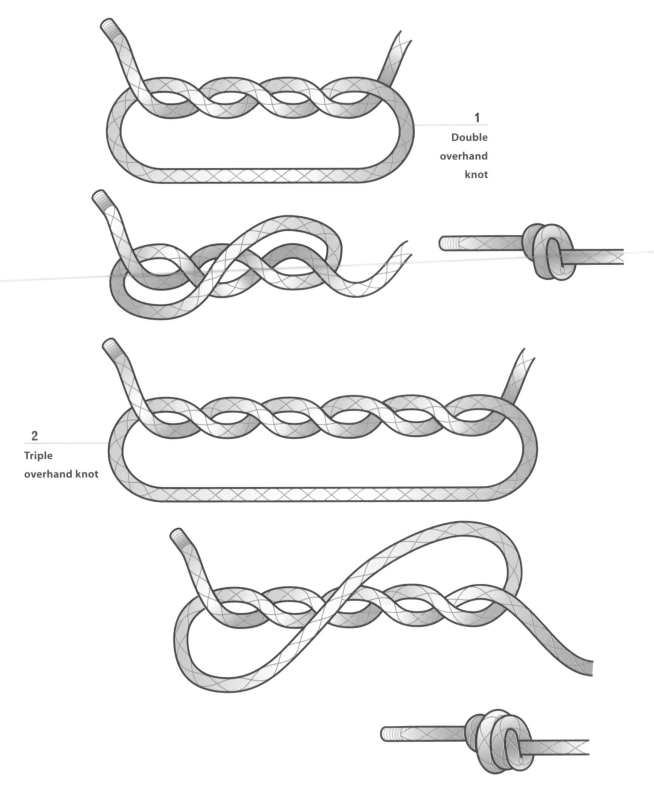

1
Double
overhand
knot

2
Triple
overhand knot

<20>

MULTIPLE OVERHAND KNOTS

A technique that must be learnt by all who tie knots – especially by anglers and climbers – is tying multiple overhand knots, also known as blood knots (from their past use by surgeons) or barrel knots (because of their shape). Tie an overhand knot, then tuck the working end a second time, for a double overhand knot (fig. 1). Begin to tighten the knot by pulling gently on both ends – feel how the knot wants to twist and wrap around itself. Allow it to do so, turning the left-hand end up and away from you, and the right-hand one down and towards you. (The instructions given here are for a right-handed knot like that shown in the diagram. They should be reversed for a formed left-handed.) Another tuck creates a triple overhand knot (fig. 2), which requires even more care in shaping the final form.

HEAT-SEALED ENDS

If a stopper knot is unwanted, you may melt and seal (by heating and cooling) the cut ends of synthetic cordage. This technique is known as heat-sealing. Be careful. If a melting gob of nylon, polyester, or whatever, sticks to you it will burn. In addition, a rough, hardened edge of cordage, clumsily handled, can lacerate skin. Apart from personal-safety considerations, heat-sealed ends may snag woven work, knitwear, etc., and some knot experts would call the practice downright shoddy workmanship. Having said this, most of us who tie knots these days sometimes resort to heat-sealing ends. Retailers can supply measured lengths of man-made cordage sealed with the aid of electrically heated guillotines, but a soldering iron with the right attachment will serve as well. The yellow flame of a match is barely hot enough for even the odd end. I often have to seal ends for craftwork, and I use the noisy blue flame on my DIY blow-torch for this purpose. Various man-made materials react differently: some melt cleanly, while others discolour. A few catch fire and burn with a small flame, which is easily blown out. You quickly learn how much heat to apply. With practice, ends

may be sealed flat or nicely rounded, or squeezed to a point (with a wetted finger and thumb).

Some tight-laid ropes unravel fast when cut. So, be prepared. First bind the rope either side of where the cut is to be made, using constrictor knots (see p. 136). Heat a knife blade until it glows red. Slice through the rope, sealing and separating both ends at once. Ends may be wrapped with adhesive tape, but is not an attractive finish. There is – I am told – one sort of tape with strengthening fibres running the length of it, which does not look out of place on ropework. Another method is to use shrinkable plastic sleeving, which comes in several diameters, from electronic accessory shops. Cut off a short length, slide it half-way over the rope's end and heat it. It may not be traditional, but if such labour-saving tricks had been possible in the past, ropeworkers would, I suspect, have been quick to adopt them.

<21>

WHIPPED ENDS

For a traditional finish, use a whipping. This should be made from natural-fibre twine for vegetable-fibre ropes, and from synthetic material for synthetics. The common whipping (figs 1-4) relies upon a pre-formed bight to pull the working end beneath and back to the middle of the wrapping turns. Leave the last round turn somewhat slack, or you will find it hard to do this, and might even break the whipping twine where the two elbows saw against one another. It is easier, I find, to bind towards the end of the rope. The time-honoured advice is to wrap against the lay of the strands, because a rope under load tends to open and this will tighten the whipping. This last tip does not apply to braided lines. On these lines, which have no spiralling furrows between strands in which the buried ends can lie, an unsightly bulge will mar the neatness of this whipping.

To pass both ends entirely through the binding turns (figs 5-7), which may be preferable, entails a modified method of tying. Either tightly

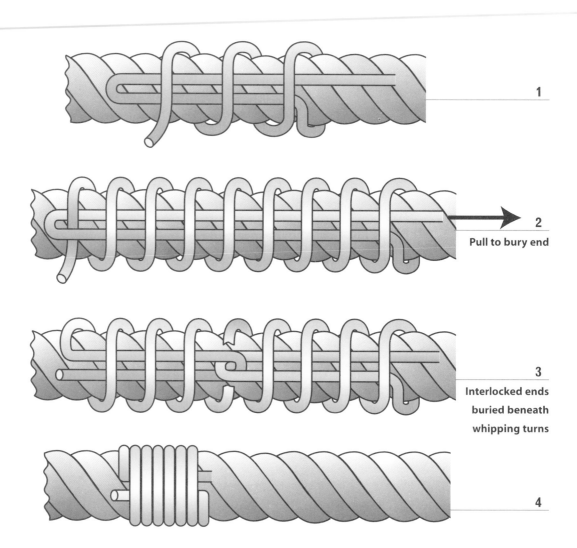

1

2
Pull to bury end

3
Interlocked ends
buried beneath
whipping turns

4

<22>

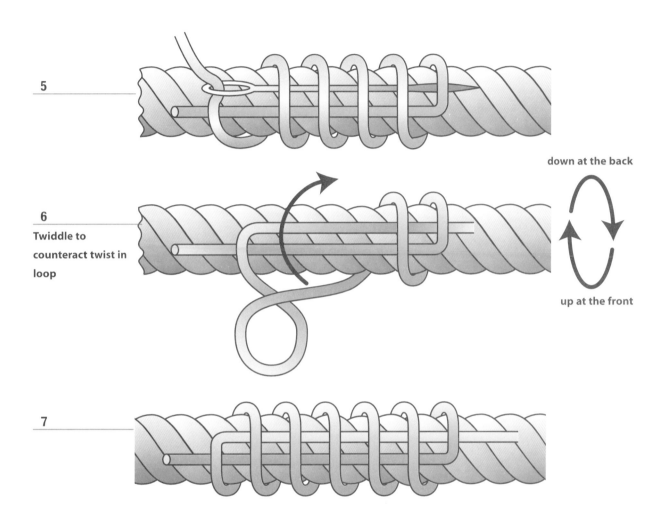

5

6

**Twiddle to
counteract twist in
loop**

down at the back

up at the front

7

wrap the twine around a needle and finish by withdrawing the needle to bury the end, or simply wrap the loop repeatedly over the end of the rope. The first time you try this you will find that twists are created in the loop, which make it harder to pull the slack through the whipping. With experience, it is possible to pre-empt this problem by putting a counter-twist into the loop before you start to wrap. This will disappear as the whipping takes shape.

1

Sailmaker's whipping

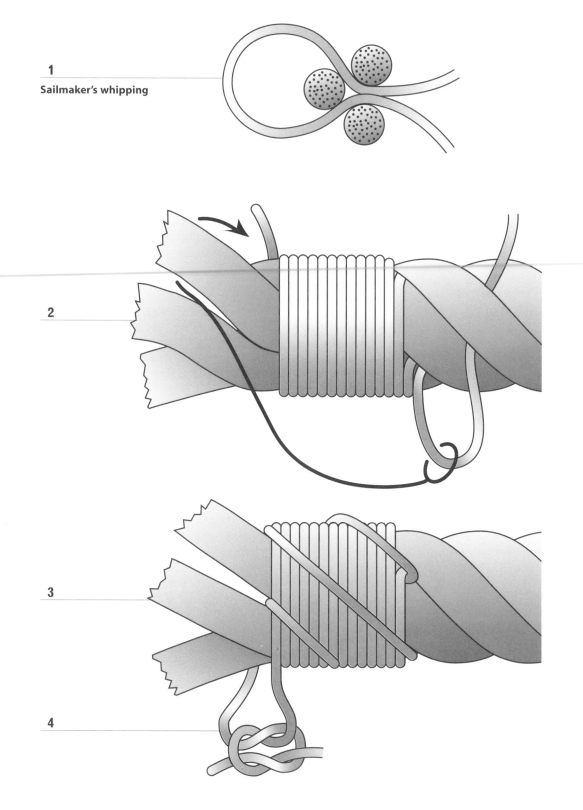

2

3

4

<24>

SAILMAKER'S WHIPPING

Most whippings will pull off if tugged hard enough. So, if the rope's end is to spend its working life being buffeted by the wind (e.g., on a flag halyard) something tenacious is needed. A sailmaker's whipping (figs 1-5) has riding turns which, on hawser-laid rope, follow the spiral grooves between the helixing strands and seize the whipping to the rope. An initial bight of twine is looped over the end of the strand it straddles, and pulled tight to enclose the completed wrapping turns. This creates two of the riding turns. Then the two ends are reef knotted to form the third. A palm-and-needle whipping like this can be stitched onto braided or sheath-and-core ropes, when it does not matter which way the riding turns are applied. For even heavier duty, on large hawsers and cables, try snaking (fig. 6).

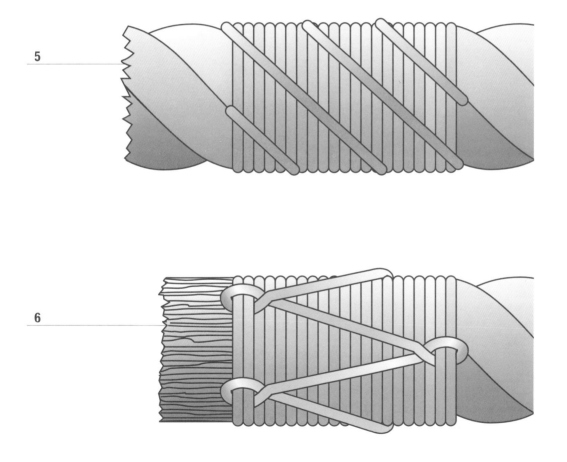

<25>

COILING

Wet ropes should be dried slowly. Keep all ropes away from abrasive dirt and grit. Do not tread on ropes. Coil them, kink-free, to carry them or hang them up. The Alpine coil (figs 1-3) is taught to climbers. Dinghy sailors and blue-water yachtsmen alike learn to put surplus sail halyard safely out from underfoot – onto the cleat or pin to which it is already made fast – with a twisted bight (figs 4-5). Storekeepers use a figure eight coil (figs 6-8 on page 28).

1

2

3

<26>

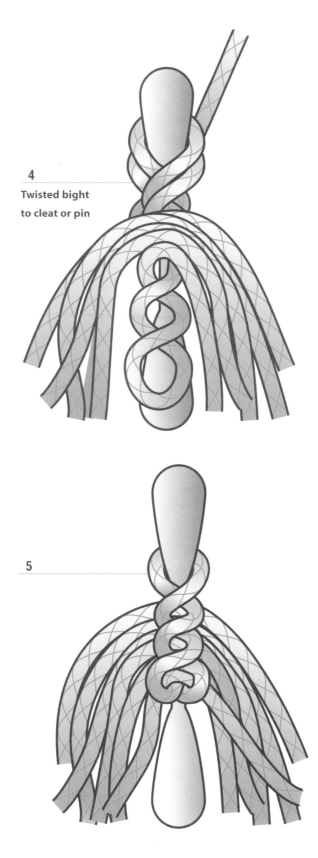

4

**Twisted bight
to cleat or pin**

5

<27>

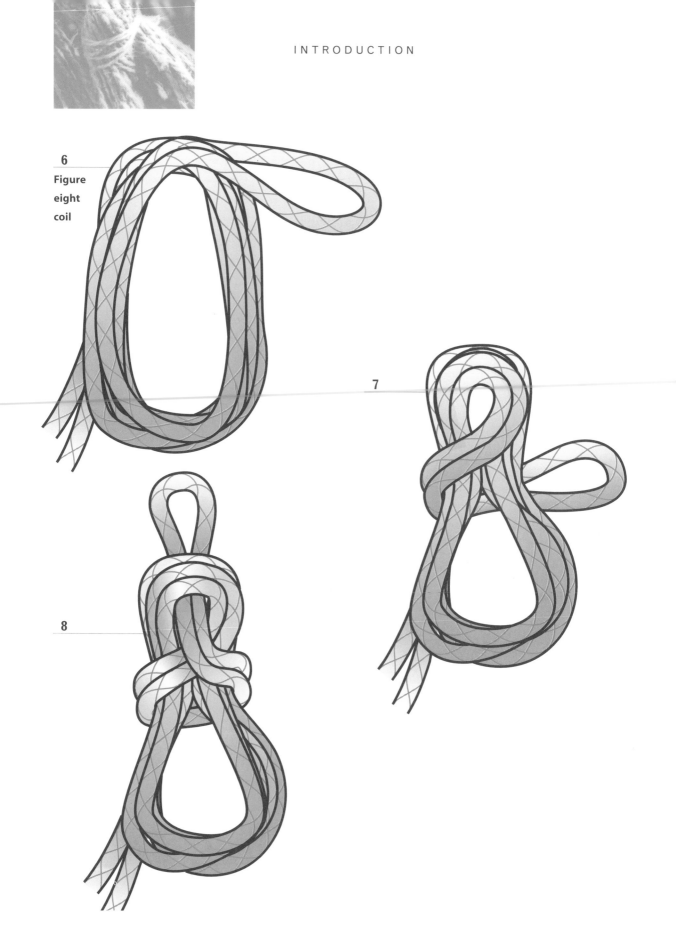

6

Figure
eight
coil

7

8

<28>

USING THE BOOK

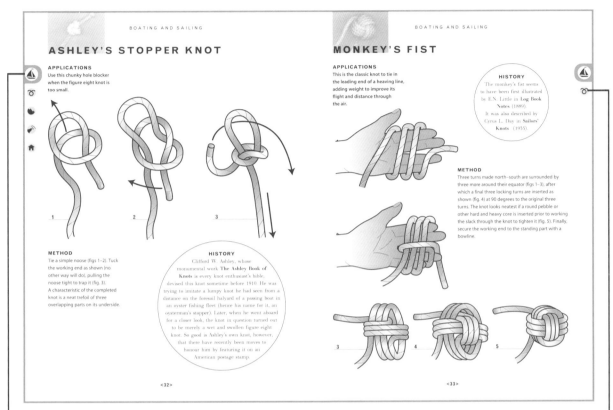

<32>

<33>

The large symbol on the thumb index at the side of every page provides an at-a-glance key that indicates both the chapter in which the knot is to be found, and the primary use for knot.

The small symbols indicate the other activities in which the knot has applications.

KEY TO THE SYMBOLS

 Boating and Sailing

 Angling and Fishing

 Outdoor Pursuits

 Home and House

 Caving and Climbing

<29>

ASHLEY'S STOPPER KNOT

APPLICATIONS

Use this chunky hole blocker when the figure eight knot is too small.

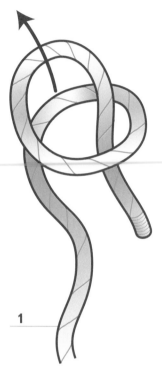

1

2

3

METHOD

Tie a simple noose (figs 1–2). Tuck the working end as shown (no other way will do), pulling the noose tight to trap it (fig. 3). A characteristic of the completed knot is a neat trefoil of three overlapping parts on its underside.

HISTORY

Clifford W. Ashley, whose monumental work **The Ashley Book of Knots** is every knot enthusiast's bible, devised this knot sometime before 1910. He was trying to imitate a lumpy knot he had seen from a distance on the foresail halyard of a passing boat in an oyster fishing fleet (hence his name for it, an oysterman's stopper). Later, when he went aboard for a closer look, the knot in question turned out to be merely a wet and swollen figure eight knot. So good is Ashley's own knot, however, that there have recently been moves to honour him by featuring it on an American postage stamp.

<32>

MONKEY'S FIST

APPLICATIONS

This is the classic knot to tie in the leading end of a heaving line, adding weight to improve its flight and distance through the air.

HISTORY

The monkey's fist seems to have been first illustrated by E.N. Little in **Log Book Notes** (1889). It was also described by Cyrus L. Day in **Sailors' Knots** (1935).

1

2

METHOD

Three turns made north–south are surrounded by three more around their equator (figs 1–3), after which a final three locking turns are inserted as shown (fig. 4) at 90 degrees to the original three turns. The knot looks neatest if a round pebble or other hard and heavy core is inserted prior to working the slack through the knot to tighten it (fig. 5). Finally, secure the working end to the standing part with a bowline.

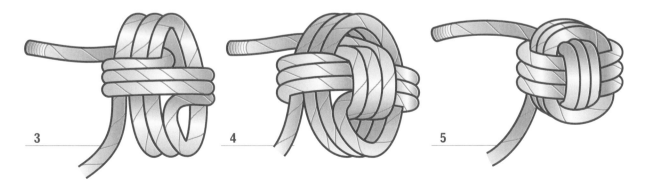

3

4

5

<33>

LAPP KNOT

APPLICATIONS

This loop knot can be used as an alternative to a bowline and also as an endless sling, a neat waist-tie or girdle, or even as an improvised safety tether.

METHOD

Make a bight in one end (fig. 1); tuck the other around and down through this (figs 2–3), ensuring that both short ends emerge on the same side of the knot (fig. 4). When tied with a draw-loop (fig. 5), the Lapp knot becomes a quick-release device. Unlike many other knots, it comes completely apart with just one tug.

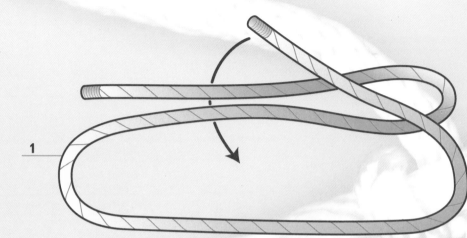

1

2

3

<34>

4

5

HISTORY

Although the Lapp knot is not
well known, it has in fact been
described since at least 1892. It has often
been called a false sheet bend, which is
perhaps why it is undervalued. Contemporary
knot researchers credited with its rehabilitation
include Pieter van de Griend (Faroe Islands),
Charles Warner (Australia) and Robert Pont
(France), who in **Knotting Matters** (April
1996) described and illustrated its use in
Lapland for tasks such as hitching
reindeer to sledges and suspending
sheath knives.

<35>

BOWLINE

APPLICATIONS

Neither a bend nor a hitch, the bowline (say 'boh-linn') is a knot that makes a fixed loop. It is far from the strongest loop knot, reducing the breaking strength of any stuff in which it is tied by as much as 40%. Nor is it very secure, particularly when the rope is stiff or slippery, when it has been known to capsize (if excessively loaded) or alternatively to spring or shake itself apart (when unloaded).

   Nevertheless the bowline can be used for a wide range of jobs, from securing the string before tying a parcel, to outdoor pursuits such as climbing. When I was a Metropolitan Police frogman in the 1960s, my colleagues and I tied the line around our waists with a simple bowline. The working end (deliberately made long) was then tucked several times around the adjacent part of the loop to secure it. Climbers' manuals advise their readers to finish off such tucks with one or two half-hitches (made in the opposite direction to the twist) for even greater security and peace of mind.

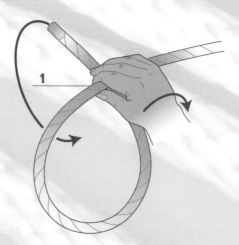

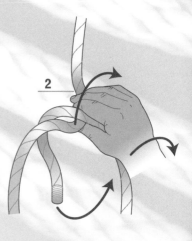

METHOD

Make it by the so-called sailor's method with a fluent, one-handed twist of the wrist (figs 1-5).

   You should also work out how to tie a bowline viewed from an unfamiliar angle (figs 6-7). Imagine facing someone, passing a rope around behind them, beneath their armpits, then having to make the knot. See what I mean? The trick is to first take a turn around the standing part of the rope with your working end. Next, pull it out straight to transfer the underhand loop in the standing part. Finally, pass and tuck the working end to lock off in the usual way.

<36>

HISTORY

Stone Age men knew the sheet bend, which has an identical layout to the bowline, the only difference being which end is used where and for what. There is, however, no evidence of the bowline having been used that far back in time. It was mentioned as a seafarer's knot by Sir Henry Mainwaring in **The Sea-man's Dictionary** (1644) and first illustrated in David Steel's **Elements and Practice of Rigging and Seamanship** in 1794. The time is long gone when it really was a 'bow line knot', used to hold the weather leech of a square sail forward closer to the wind, preventing it being pulled back. Other nautical uses include looping a boat's painter or ship's mooring rope around a quayside bollard, and tying a line around a crewman's waist, to lower him over the side. Two interlocked bowlines also form a handy hawser bend. Some useful variants on the common bowline (e.g., a double bowline, a bowline in the bight and a couple of triple bowlines) also appear in this book. All, however, rely upon you first mastering the basic knot.

8

9

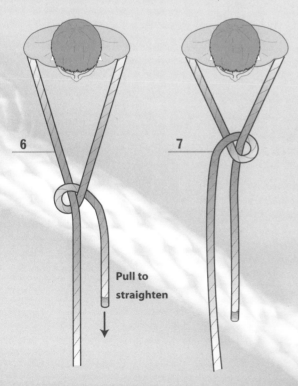

6

7

Pull to straighten

If the knot will have to withstand rough treatment, tie the double bowline (figs 8-9). This has a breaking strength of 70–75% and is therefore stronger and far more secure than a basic bowline.

<37>

BOWLINE IN THE BIGHT

APPLICATIONS

In these litigious, health-and-safety conscious times, I do not recommend any **ad hoc** rope slings and chairs for working aloft or over the side. There are tested and certificated ladders and stages and harnesses for the well-prepared. But all sailors sooner or later are faced with some urgent improvisation. This is one such knot, which can be used for lowering an injured person and other emergencies. One leg is put through each loop and the patient (if conscious and capable) holds tight onto the rope at chest level, or is somehow secured to it. It reduces the strength of the line in which it is tied by up to 40%.

METHOD

As this knot is usually tied in the middle of a rope, it must be made without using either end. The early stages are done with a doubled end (fig. 1). The trick is then to pass the bight right over the pre-formed knot (figs 2-3).

1

2

3

HISTORY

This knot was illustrated in 1795 by Johann Röding in his **Allgemeines Wörterbuch der Marine**. In 1808 it was mentioned as the 'bowline upon the bight' by Darcy Lever, author of **Sheet Anchor**.

<38>

FISHERMAN'S KNOT

APPLICATIONS

This is – strictly speaking – a strong and secure bend to join two similar ropes.

METHOD

Lay the two working parts alongside and parallel to one another (fig. 1). Tie an identical overhand knot around each standing part with the other working end (figs 2–3). Pull them together (figs 4–5).

HISTORY

In the early nineteenth century, fishermen referred to this knot as the water knot. It has also been known as the angler's knot, the English knot, the Englishman's knot, the true lover's knot and the waterman's knot. The author Captain Marryat wrote of it in his novel **Peter Simple** (1834): '... there is a moral in that knot ... that points out the necessity of pulling together ... when we wish to hold on.'

1

2

3

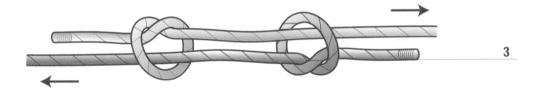

4

Front view

5

Back view

<39>

SHEET BEND

APPLICATIONS

The sheet bend is a general-purpose bend for uniting two lines made of the same material. It may also be used to attach an end to a loop or small eye. It does, however, have a number of limitations. It will jam under a heavy load and, without an extra tuck, can slip in smooth materials. Security tests have shown it to spill after an average 22 tugs out of 100, and it is not a very strong knot, with a breaking strength of 55%.

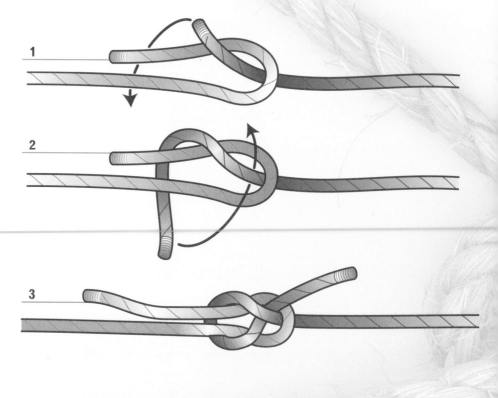

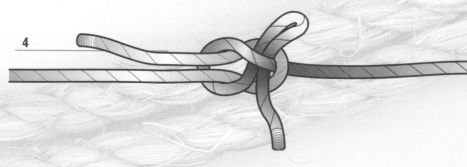

METHOD

As a general rule, aim to keep both short ends on the same side (figs 1–3). Leave a draw-loop if you prefer (fig. 4). For ropes of different size, composition or wetness, use the double sheet bend (fig. 5), when the smaller and more flexible cordage makes the double turn around the thicker bight. If the knot is to be subjected to rough treatment, consider reinforcing it with a backward tuck (fig. 6), which also makes it more streamline and easier to pull one way through narrow gaps. Swedish marine writer and artist Frank Rosenow spotted a sheet bend in Greek cruising waters used as a bridle for three converging ropes (fig. 7).

<40>

HISTORY

The sheet bend was probably known by Neolithic people; remnants of Stone Age nets have been found with mesh knots resembling sheet bends. David Steel referred to it by this name in **Elements and Practice of Rigging and Seamanship** (1794), when it was tied in a sheet (i.e., a bit of running rigging to trim a sail). Many knot experts campaign against the use of this bend for lines of different size, pointing out that (if they are too dissimilar) a thick and stiff rope could straighten out and spill the small cord. While this is a fair criticism, the sheet bend — if used sensibly — cannot simply be dismissed.

5

Double sheet bend

6

One-way (back-tucked) sheet bend

7

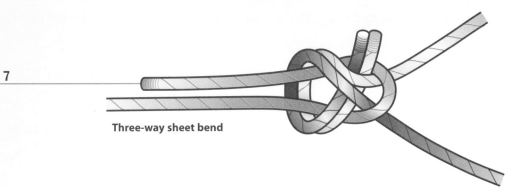

Three-way sheet bend

<41>

SEIZING BEND

APPLICATIONS

When two lines are too dissimilar for a sheet bend to be relied on, use a seizing bend instead. It is ideal when using a lightweight throwing line as the messenger to haul a heavier working rope into position. It is a strong and secure bend that, having been subjected to all kinds of use, or misuse, can be easily untied.

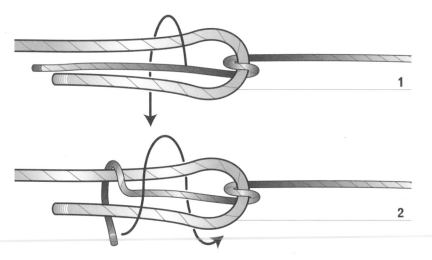

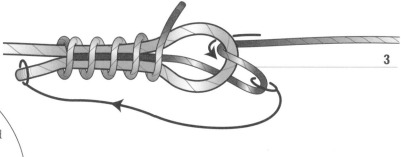

HISTORY

Knotting innovator Harry Asher created the seizing bend and first described it in **A New System of Knotting** (published in 1986 by the International Guild of Knot Tyers). It was later included in **Knotting Matters** (October 1989).

METHOD

Form a bight in the bigger of the two lines (fig. 1). Take a turn with the thin cord and bring the ensuing wrapping turns up **towards** the bight end (fig. 2). The initial turn is now extended and looped over the short end of the larger rope (fig. 3) to become a frapping (tensioning) turn holding everything in place. Even in this unfinished form the knot is secure enough for many purposes. A heavy-duty version can be made by fixing the free end to the standing part with a bowline (fig. 4). To loosen both versions, just yank up on the short working end. The part holding down the turns may now be further raised and the knot undone.

<42>

CARRICK BEND

APPLICATIONS

This is a bend for joining larger ropes and cables. Although often assumed to be strong, it is in fact only about 65% efficient.

METHOD

Weave the ropes over and under, as shown in figs 1–2. Arrange the layout so that the working ends emerge on opposite sides of the knot. Pull the knot tight, capsizing it into its stable working form (fig. 3). The version with both short ends on the same side (fig. 4) may be less secure and so is not recommended as a bend. (However, it is a crucial knot for students of mathematical knot theory, which is beyond the scope of this book.) Bring the working end around to re-enter the knot (fig. 5), doubling and trebling the lead, to make a decorative Turk's head mat or bracelet.

1

2

3

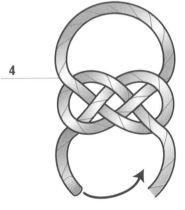

4

5

HISTORY

The symmetrical layout of the carrick bend, with eight crossing points, yields several different knots, depending on what goes over and under where. For this reason, some very unreliable knots have been misleadingly labelled carrick bends. The true carrick bend was named by M. Lescallier in **Vocabulaire des Termes de Marine** (1783) and featured by Felix Reisenberg in **Seamanship for the Merchant Service** (1922). The name 'carrick' may come from medieval trading ships called carracks.

<43>

ZEPPELIN BEND

APPLICATIONS

This is probably the best of a whole trustworthy family of symmetrical bends comprising two interlocked overhand knots. It works even in big stiff hawsers and cables and is suitable for everything from hobbies to heavy industrial use.

METHOD

Rosendahl's tying method is a trifle awkward and so an easier way (figs 1–3) has been devised by Ettrick W. Thomson of Suffolk, England. The knot does not have to be completely tightened before loading; it is secure even with daylight showing through it (fig. 4). To untie the knot, push and pull on the twin encircling bights – tap them with a mallet if necessary – until some slack is obtained. Then, bit by bit, loosen the whole arrangement. It is possible to untie Zeppelin bends that have borne loads of several hundred tonnes.

1

2

3

4

5

HISTORY

Lee and Bob Payne revealed in **Boating magazine** ('The Forgotten Zeppelin Knot', March 1976) that this knot was used by the US Navy until 1962 to tether its lighter-than-air ships. Able Seaman Joe Collins, a marlinspike seamanship instructor in the 1930s, told the Paynes how he had served under American aeronaut hero Lieutenant Commander Charles Rosendahl, skipper of the dirigible **Los Angeles**: 'There was only one knot he allowed … either for bending lines together on the airship or for use on the mooring lines. I called it the Rosendahl bend.'

<44>

KNUTE HITCH

APPLICATIONS

Use the Knute hitch to attach a line to anything with a hole not much larger (for obvious reasons) than twice the diameter of the cordage used. This hitch is often tied to fix lanyards to knives and other tools. Europe's largest sailing school, in Poole Harbour, England, uses it to attach the main halyards to the mainsails on its Wayfarer dinghies, no doubt saving on the cost of shackles lost overboard from wet, cold and inexperienced fingers.

METHOD

Thread a bight and trap the working end with it (fig. 1), finishing off either with a stopper knot or with one of those big plastic beads sold in yacht chandlers (fig. 2).

1

Stopper knot

2

HISTORY

US master rigger, writer and broadcaster Brion Toss named this hitch in 1990 but it is probably centuries old.

<45>

MOORING HITCH

APPLICATIONS

This is a versatile slide-and-grip knot, with the extra facility of a quick-release draw-loop. It will moor a dinghy, tether a docile animal and act as the DIY enthusiast's occasional 'third hand'.

HISTORY

The history of the mooring hitch is anybody's guess. Mine is that it could have been a medieval archer's adjustable bowstring knot.

1

2

METHOD

Tying the mooring hitch is simplicity itself (figs 1–2), with the draw-loop making an over-under-over locking tuck.

<46>

KILLICK HITCH

APPLICATIONS

Use the killick hitch to tow long loads through water or drag them overland. It works well on rough objects, such as tree trunks, but can slip on smooth spars. (See also icicle hitch, p. 70.)

Method

Begin by making a timber hitch (fig. 1). Three tucks or turns were enough to do this using vegetable-fibre rope but more may be prudent when using today's smoother braids. In hawser-laid rope it is traditional to dog the turns the same way as the lay. Arrange the direction of pull to preserve the twist of the timber hitch. I personally always make the half-hitch so that the end emerges the same way as it does from the initial knot (fig. 2). Note that the half-hitch, with its elbows, almost certainly reduces the breaking strength (70%) of the initial timber hitch.

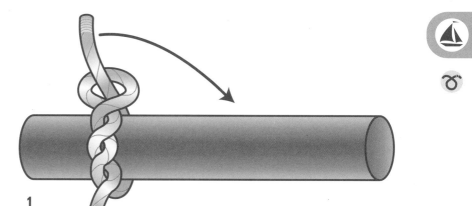

1

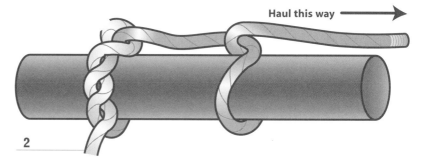

Haul this way ⟶

2

HISTORY

The killick is essentially a timber hitch with an additional half-hitch to give direction to the line of pull. The timber hitch is an old knot, mentioned in **A Treatise on Rigging** (c. 1625) and illustrated by Denis Diderot in his **Encyclopédie** of 1762. It has been used since time immemorial. The killick hitch was illustrated and named by David Steel in **Elements and Practice of Rigging and Seamanship** (1794), a **killick** being a naval term for a small anchor (or even a rock used as one). Thus the killick hitch used to be an anchor knot for a boat, buoy or lobster pot.

<47>

CLOVE HITCH

APPLICATIONS

This simple but versatile knot will moor a small boat, suspend a fender or attach any line to a post, rail or ring when the pull is a steady one at right-angles to the point of attachment. However, simplicity has its shortcomings. If pulled around, the clove hitch can work loose. Perversely, it can also jam when wet. Its breaking strength is variously quoted as between 60% and 75%.

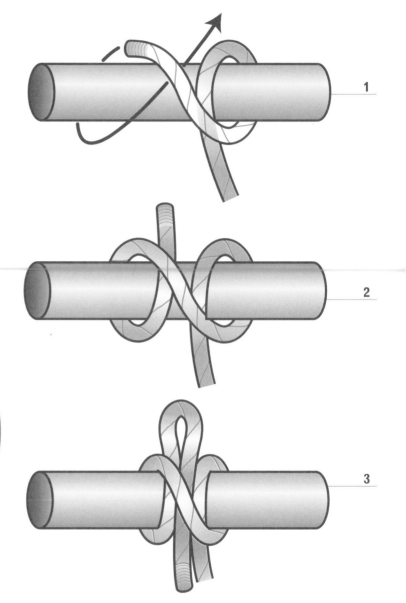

1

2

3

HISTORY

An old treatise referred to this knot as a builder's knot. William Falconer may have been the first to name it the clove hitch in his **Universal Dictionary of the Marine** (1769). Aboard ship it was used to secure ratlines to shrouds, creating those rope ladders up which sailormen scrambled to man the yardarms.

METHOD

This knot can be tied by tracing a letter N (or its mirror image) with the working end (figs 1–2). For a temporary task, such as hanging a fender, leave a draw-loop (fig. 3). Stepping ashore from a slow-moving boat, first cast an underhand loop onto a bollard and use the friction to check the momentum; then, once the line is the length you want it, simply drop the second loop onto the first. Add a half-hitch for extra security. To ensure the direction of pull on a mooring painter does not vary, bring it ashore around a stanchion or other convenient fixed point before attaching it to a post or rail.

<48>

ROLLING HITCH

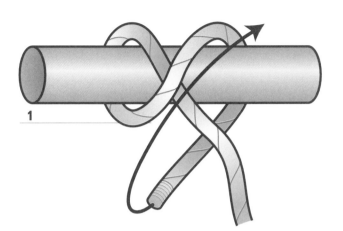

1

APPLICATIONS
A close relation of the clove hitch (see p. 48), the rolling hitch attaches a cord to a rope for a lengthwise pull. For smooth rails or spars, consider using the icicle hitch (see p. 70).

METHOD
Begin as for the clove hitch (fig. 1) but take two adjacent diagonal turns on the side of the knot from which the pull will come (figs 2–3). Take care to lock the second diagonal turn inside the first one, i.e., alongside the standing part of the line.

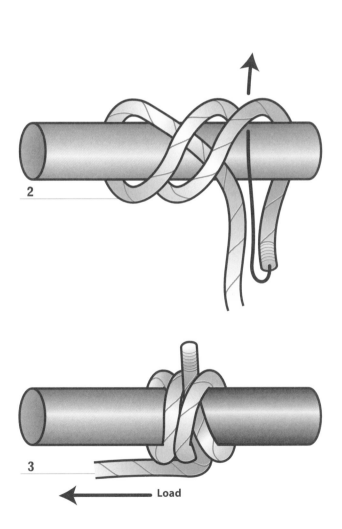

2

3

← **Load**

HISTORY
This knot was known in earlier days as Magner's hitch or the Magnus hitch.

<49>

SNUGGLE HITCH

APPLICATIONS

Useful for attaching a line to a spar or rope, the snuggle hitch is stronger than either the clove or rolling hitches (see pp. 48 and 49). It may be used with a right-angled or a lengthwise pull.

HISTORY

The snuggle hitch was devised by Owen K. Nuttall of West Yorkshire, England, and was first published in **Knotting Matters** in January 1987.

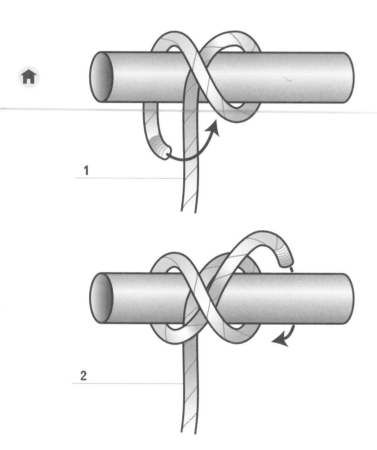

1

2

3

METHOD

For a lengthwise pull, ensure that the two adjacent wrapping turns are on the same side of the standing part as the load (figs 1-3). Once the load is released, the knot may be untied by either pulling or prising loose the part arrowed (fig. 4). The working end can then be withdrawn.

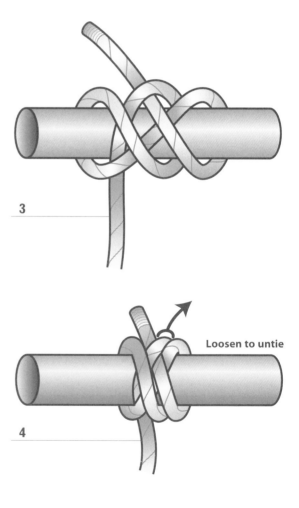

Loosen to untie

4

<50>

BUNTLINE HITCH

APPLICATIONS

The buntline hitch was traditionally used to secure a lanyard to a cringle, eyelet, ring or swivel. These days it is also used on tools with small holes in their handles. Note the short end trapped on the inside of the knot (fig. 3). This is not recommended in cases where the hitch needs to be undone easily, because it is likely to jam and resist the efforts of fingers to free it. However, where something more secure than the normal two half-hitches is needed, the buntline hitch is useful. When tied in a strip of material, it turns out to be the common knot used for men's neckties (one of life's lesser-known trivial facts).

METHOD

Make two half-hitches, tying the second inside the first (figs 1–3).

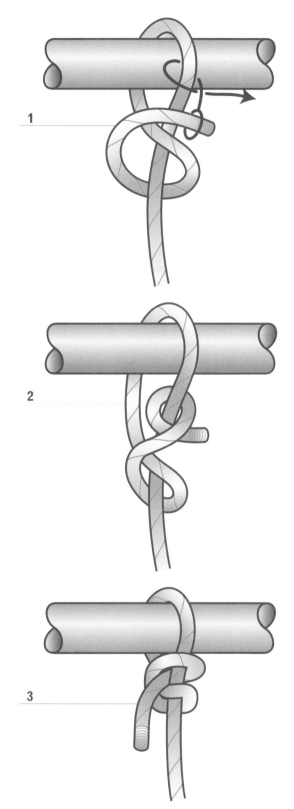

1

2

3

HISTORY

The buntline was attached to a sail's footrope, then passed up in front of that sail to a block on the yard, from where it could be used to pull the bottom of the sail up and so spill the wind out of it. As the sail was going to flap about a lot, a very secure knot was needed.

<51>

ROUND TURN & TWO HALF-HITCHES

APPLICATIONS

This is a classic old hitch for securing a line to a ring, rail or to a spar. (See also anchor bend, p. 53.)

(See also anchor bend, p. 53.)

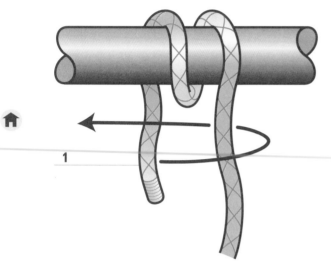

HISTORY

In 1794 David Steel referred to this hitch (by the same name) in **Elements and Practice of Rigging and Seamanship.**

1

METHOD

Use the friction of the round turn (fig. 1) to snub and hold the load; then add the two identical half-hitches (figs 2–3). The two half-hitches have a breaking strength of 60–75%, but the round turn may increase that percentage.

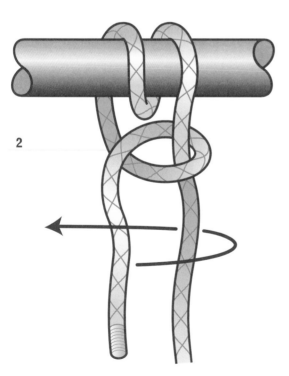

2

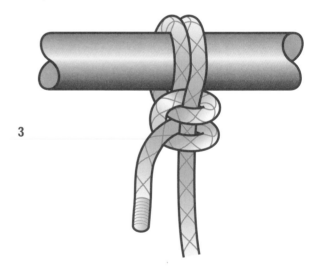

3

<52>

ANCHOR BEND

Applications

Used on small boats for securing rope warps to anchor rings, this knot is misleadingly named. It is actually a strong-ish (70–75%) and secure hitch for wet and slimy conditions.

Method

Take a round turn but then pass the first of two identical half-hitches through it (figs 1–3). The 1904 variant (fig. 4) is a round turn through a round turn, which, when it has been systematically worked up snug, makes a semi-permanent knot.

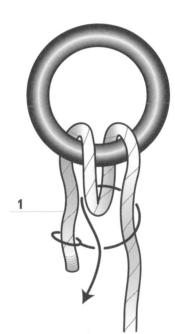

1

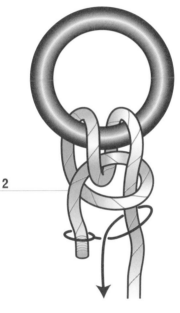

2

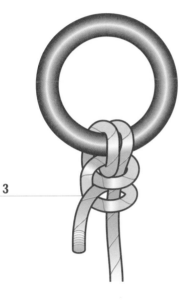

3

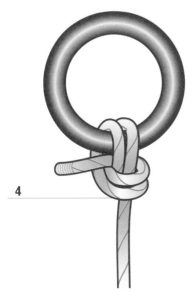

4

HISTORY

The anchor bend was recommended by David Steel in **Elements and Practice of Rigging and Seamanship** (1794). It is also known as the fisherman's bend. A neat variant appeared in the anonymous **Handbook of Boat Sailing** (1904).

<53>

LIGHTERMAN'S HITCH

APPLICATIONS

When tied around a towing post or hook, this is a superb hitch for securing one boat, barge or ship to another. It also serves to belay a heavy-duty ship's mooring or a marquee guy-line. Whatever the use, it will hold fast, but it cannot jam and is quickly cast off.

1

Load

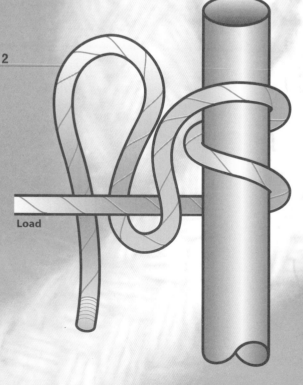

2

Load

METHOD

Take a turn (or two or three) to apply whatever friction the job demands (fig. 1). Once the strain is taken up and the line length adjusted for the job in hand, take a bight beneath the standing part and hitch it over the post, bollard or stake (figs 2–3). Wrap the end around once and let it hang (fig. 4).

<54>

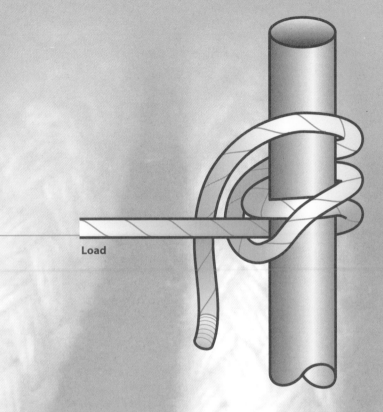

3

Load

4

Load

HISTORY

Seamanship manuals
overlook this most practical of
hitches. Riggers (in the circus and
theatre, as well as afloat), lightermen
and watermen have known and used it for
generations. In my work as a crew member on
board a Thames Police duty boat, I towed
laden lighters weighing several hundred
tonnes with a line attached this way.
Clifford Ashley in **The Ashley Book
of Knots** (1944) referred to this
hitch as the backhanded
mooring hitch.

<55>

HEAVING LINE KNOT

APPLICATIONS
Throwing lines fly better through the air if the end is weighted, and this is one knot for the job. (See also monkey's fist, p. 33.) Tied in a length of cord it makes a neat, convenient hank to carry in a rucksack or on a belt loop.

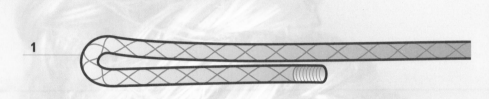

METHOD
Make a bight and wrap the two adjacent parts with the working end (figs 1–2). After tucking the working end, pull all slack through the knot (first one way, then the other) until it emerges where the standing part enters the knot (figs 3–4). For a bulkier version of the same knot, wrap three standing parts (figs 5–7).

<58>

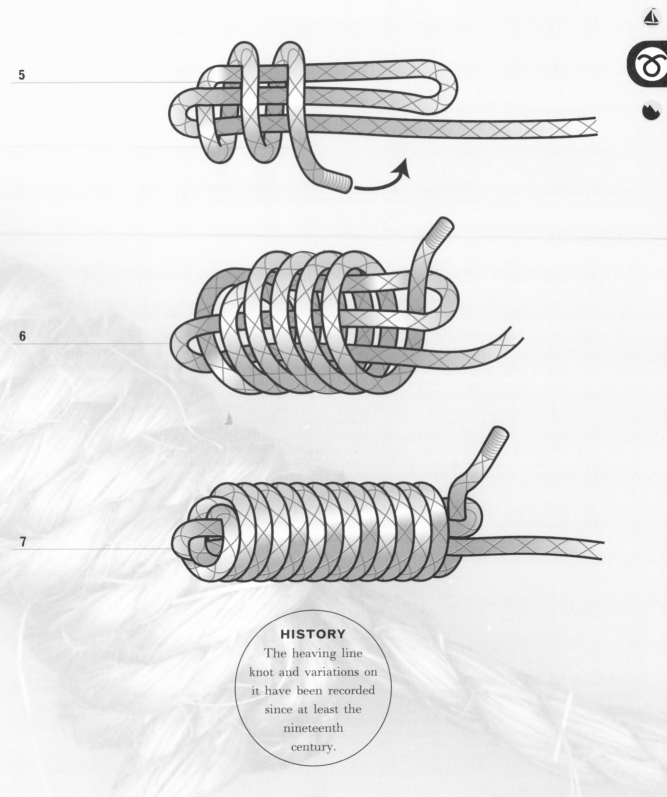

5

6

7

HISTORY

The heaving line knot and variations on it have been recorded since at least the nineteenth century.

<59>

BOA KNOT

APPLICATIONS

The ultimate binding,
this neatly combines
the forms and functions
of both constrictor and
strangle knots. It may
be tied in the same size
of cord around a wide
range of diameters,
wherever seizing or
lashing is needed.

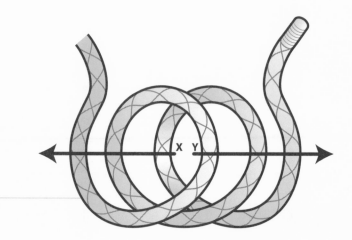

1

METHOD

Lay down two right-handed,
overhand loops, one on top of the
other (figs 1-2). Then simply twist
the resulting coil into the figure
eight layout shown, and slide the
knot onto its foundation (fig. 3).
Draw it up snug, neatening any
misaligned cord parts as you do so
(fig. 4). The knot will usually be tied
in the bight like this. It may be
formed with a working end by first
tying a basic constrictor knot (fig. 5)
and then wrapping and tucking
one of the ends as shown (figs 6-7).

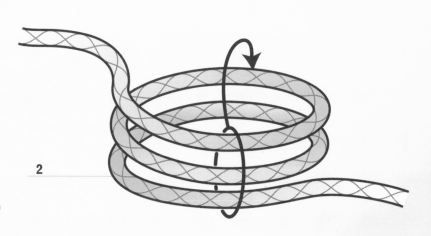

2

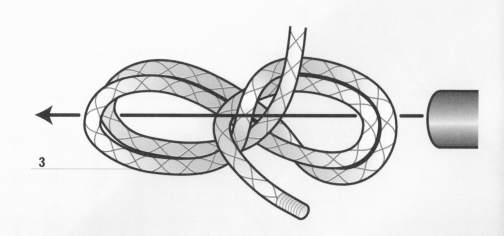

3

HISTORY

This — the newest knot in the book — was discovered in 1996 by Dr Peter Collingwood, the eminent weaver and craft writer, in his search for a reliable seizing on ends which had to be cut very short; and it is a nice example of how knots emerge to fill what (with hindsight) is an obvious gap in the family tree but was previously an overlooked and unsuspected missing link. I have added this superb knot to my own repertoire and recommend it.

4

5

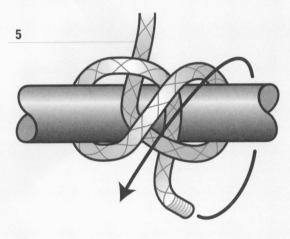

6

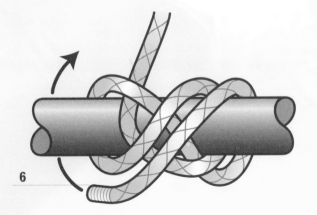

7

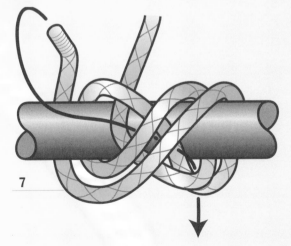

<61>

BOWSTRING KNOT AND LOOP

APPLICATIONS

When tension is a critical factor, this adjustable loop will tighten or slacken tent guy-lines, temporary washing lines, etc.

METHOD

Tuck the working end through the overhand knot (figs 1–2). There is only one correct way – and five wrong ways – to do this. Add a stopper knot (fig. 3) for extra security. The Oriental alternative (figs 4–6) incorporates an extra piece of cord and was designed for a cord that ends in a bight or loop.

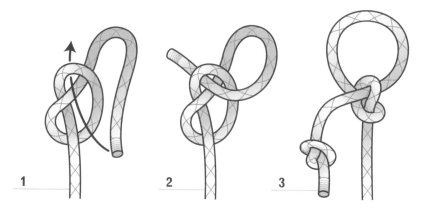

1

2

3

4

5

6

HISTORY

Elizabethan archers looped the tops of their bowstrings and tightened them with this knot; but it was used by the indigenous peoples of several continents and so is no doubt much older. I have seen something similar as a ligature around the neck of a mummified Ancient Briton (c. 500 BC). Spanish vaqueros and American cowboys, who used it in their lariats, called it a honda knot.

<62>

MANHARNESS KNOT

APPLICATIONS

This knot is used to put a shoulder loop in a rope when hauling a load.

METHOD

Make a large loop and pull a bight through under-over (figs 1–3). The load should be applied in the direction shown (fig. 4).

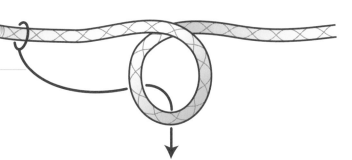

1

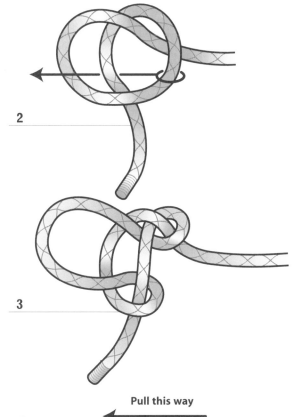

2

3

Pull this way

4

HISTORY

The manharness knot's other names – the artilleryman's loop, the harness loop and the manharness hitch – indicate its earlier uses for lugging field guns into position and easing the strain on horses struggling uphill or in muddy going. Indeed, in 1887 the British Army called it 'a man's harness hitch' (**Instruction in Military Engineering**). Boy Scouts were once taught to put these knots in the drag lines of their trek carts.

In **Knotting Matters** (April 1992) Mike Storch recommended using a series of manharness knots at intervals along a picket line to tether horses.

<63>

SCAFFOLD KNOT

APPLICATIONS

This is a tough noose knot, which may be protected against wear due to chafing by the insertion of a plastic or metal lining called a thimble, creating what sailors refer to as a 'hard eye'. Thimbles come in a range of sizes and are obtainable from boat and yacht chandlers. Practised fingers can tie the scaffold knot in 30 seconds or less.

METHOD

First make the loop and tighten the sliding knot (figs 1–3). Next, insert the thimble (fig. 4). See that its jaws bed down into the throat of the noose and pull the whole lot snug. To attach a line directly to a ring or bracket, without using a shackle, fix the thimble in place and pass the working end of the line around it before tying the knot.

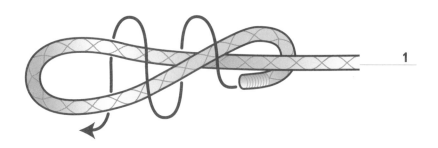

1

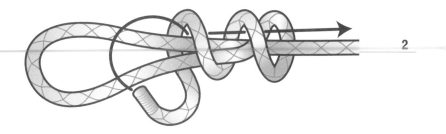

2

3

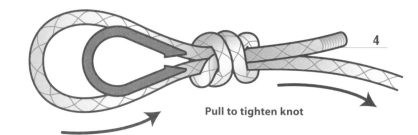

4

Pull to tighten knot

HISTORY

The scaffold knot was described in Denis Diderot's **Encyclopédie** of 1762.

<64>

MIDSHIPMAN'S HITCH

APPLICATIONS

Primarily an adjustable loop for moorings, guy-lines, etc., the midshipman's hitch has even been suggested (minus the final half-hitch) as a quick way to attach yourself to a life-line in an emergency. In a situation of this kind, grip the working end to the standing part with at least one hand.

METHOD

Tie a rolling hitch (see p. 49) onto the standing part of the line (figs 1–4). Carefully arranged, it should neither slip nor jam. To make the hitch semi–permanent, tape or knot the end to the adjacent rope.

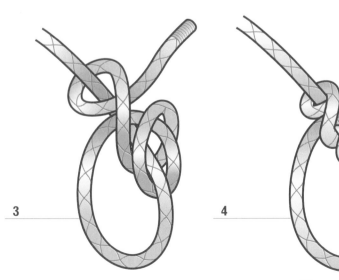

1

2

3

4

HISTORY

The name of this early slide-and-grip knot suggests a naval origin, and, as the rank of midshipman was a lowly one, it may be that it was a derogatory term for an underrated knot.

<65>

HANDCUFF KNOT

APPLICATIONS
A fireman's chair knot (see p. 148) can be started with this knot, which can also hobble a live animal, sling a carcass or render an escapologist helpless.

METHOD
Interweave two mirror-image loops under and over each other (figs 1–2). Alternatively, pull straight through (figs 3–4) into the simpler six crossing-point knot called the Tom fool's knot. Some feel this is inferior to the handcuff knot, with its eight crossing points, but there is evidence to show one is more or less as good as the other.

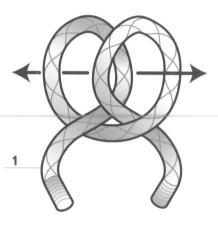

1

2

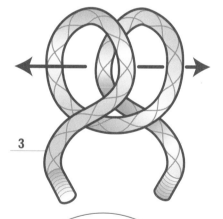

3

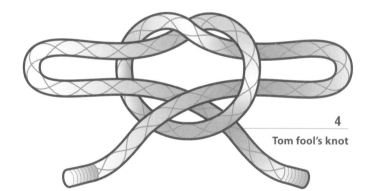

4

Tom fool's knot

HISTORY
So-called handcuff knots may have originated, as an alternative to a picket line, to prevent grazing animals straying from overnight camps.

<66>

TARBUCK KNOT

APPLICATIONS

A useful general-purpose slide-and-grip loop, the Tarbuck knot may be grasped in the hand and shifted along, but it will seize up under load. It is used to tension guy-lines, clothes-lines, etc., and can also be used to moor small craft temporarily on a rising or falling tide.

Method

Take two and a half turns with the working end around the standing part, bringing it out through the loop so formed (figs 1-2). Then twist the working end in a figure eight around the standing part and under itself, as shown (fig 3). There is only one right way to tie this knot but many wrong ways. Work the entire knot snug before use. Do not use this knot as a hitch around a rigid rope or rail to resist a lengthwise pull (illustrated in at least one manual). It seems like a good idea, but it should be remembered that the knot relies for its grip on creating a dog's-leg kink in its own standing part (fig. 4). This is impossible if the line is tied to a separate and unyielding foundation.

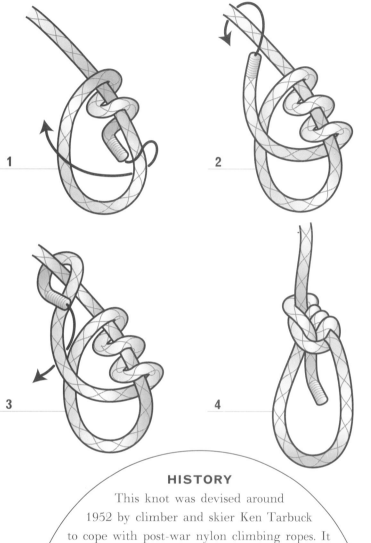

1

2

3

4

HISTORY

This knot was devised around 1952 by climber and skier Ken Tarbuck to cope with post-war nylon climbing ropes. It was an end man's tie-on to a karabiner, intended to absorb sudden loads by slipping until the load was reduced to a safe weight (when the knot would hold). But no sooner had it become widely known through Tarbuck's expert writing and lecturing, than kernmantel (core-sheath) climbing ropes emerged. These absorb shock loading by their elasticity and the Tarbuck knot can ruin such ropes, gripping and stripping the outer sheath. It is therefore no longer recommended for its original specialized purpose.

<67>

VICE VERSA

APPLICATIONS

This is a tight bend for slippery cordage, especially useful in wet conditions.

METHOD

The interweaving (figs 1–4) is not too hard to follow, although every crossing point over and under must be exactly right. The appearance of the finished knot (fig. 5) is distinctive.

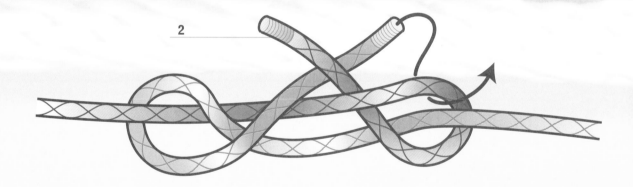

<68>

HISTORY

Retired research scientist Harry Asher discovered this knot while working systematically through derivations from the common sheet bend. It was published by him in **The Alternative Knot Book** (1989). Asher was, however, unaware that his knot was perhaps much earlier in origin. When the writer and traveller Tim Severin started to make his replica of the cow-hide boat used by the sixth-century Irish monk St Brendan, he found that the wet leather thongs with which he was working were like slippery snakes, pulling out of any knot he tried. Eventually, with a lot of twisting and interlacing, he made a knot that held. As he wrote in 1978 in the **Sunday Times Magazine**: '... in a curious way [the knot] looked much like the braided patterns found in Irish manuscript illustrations.' And it might have looked much like this knot too.

4

5

<69>

ICICLE HITCH

APPLICATIONS

The icicle hitch can attach a line to the smoothest of spars or rails (including a polished brass fireman's pole), even when it tapers towards the direction of pull.

1

2

3

Pull to tighten

4

METHOD

A. End of spar accessible

Take at least four turns around the rail or spar (fig. 1); take more if an exceptionally secure hitch is required. With the working end, create a generous loop hanging down behind the standing part (fig. 2). Pass this loop in front of all other parts and drop it, without twisting, over the end of the spar (fig 3). Draw everything up tight by pulling first the standing part and then the working end at right-angles to the spar. Now tighten it all again. Only then can the load be carefully applied, and the knot pulled out to the shape shown (fig. 4). There must be no separation of the two turns on the thicker part of the spar. If this occurs, add extra turns at the start. As long as two turns on the thicker part remain snug together, the hitch should hold fast.

<70>

5

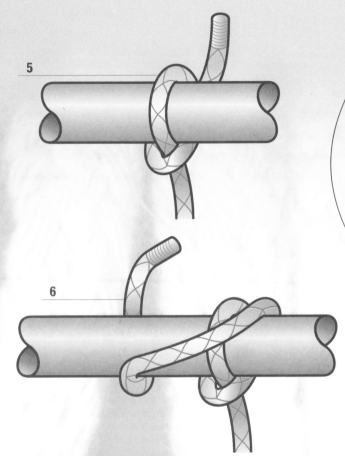

6

HISTORY

An extended pile hitch (see p. 72), the icicle hitch was devised by John Smith of Surrey, England. He demonstrated his knot's quite exceptional grip in May 1990 at the eighth Annual General Meeting of the International Guild of Knot Tyers, held at the training ship **Steadfast**, a Sea Cadet shore establishment at Farnham in Hampshire. Smith hung by this hitch from a splicing fid, which was suspended, point down, from the ceiling.

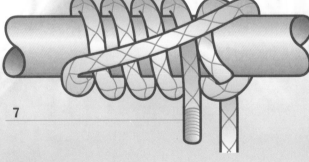

7

B. End of spar inaccessible

Using the working end, assemble the knot as shown (figs 5–8), but then tighten it until it behaves as already detailed in A above.

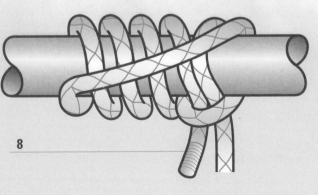

8

<71>

PILE HITCH

APPLICATIONS

This hitch is used for making a line fast to a stake, post, pile or bollard. It is best tied in the bight.

1

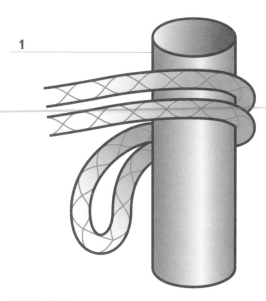

2

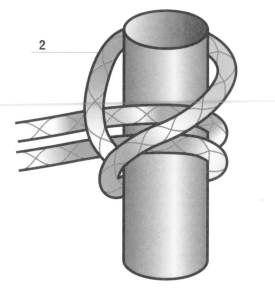

METHOD

Take a turn with a bight beneath the standing part and place it over the post, etc. (figs 1–3).

3

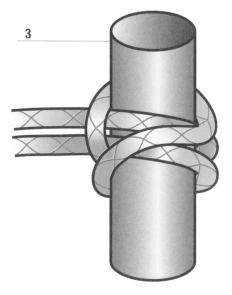

<72>

HIGHWAYMAN'S HITCH

APPLICATIONS

A temporary tether for an animal or for mooring a boat, the highwayman's hitch may be tied in the bight of a middled rope, so that a long end is within reach to undo it again. This knot can be used to hold almost anything that will have to be released quickly or awkwardly (e.g., with one hand, or with the teeth, or from a distance).

METHOD

This is the ultimate in draw-loop knots, tied simply by making one loop on top of another (figs 1–4).

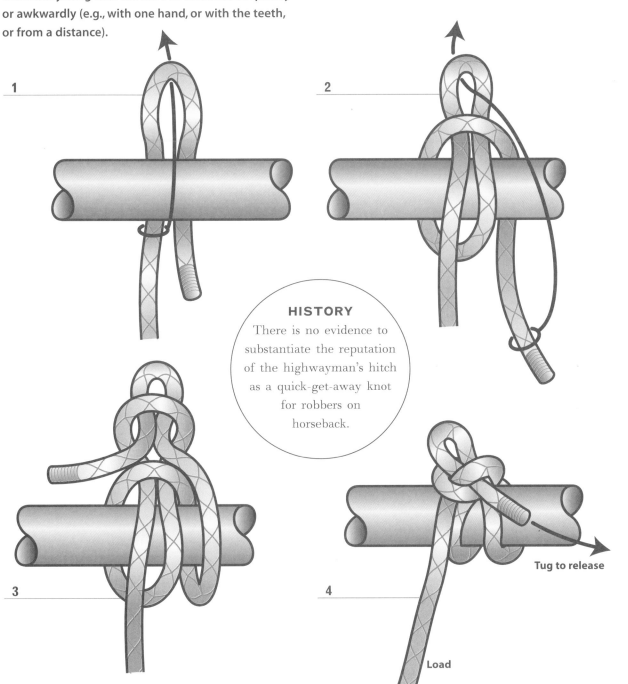

1

2

HISTORY

There is no evidence to substantiate the reputation of the highwayman's hitch as a quick-get-away knot for robbers on horseback.

3

4

Tug to release

Load

<73>

POLE HITCH

APPLICATIONS
The pole hitch is a gathering and binding knot. A pair of these will hold assorted long objects.

HISTORY
In 1987 this hitch was recommended by the Girl Guides Association for lashing tent poles together. (See **Knotting for Guides** by Hazel Bailey.)

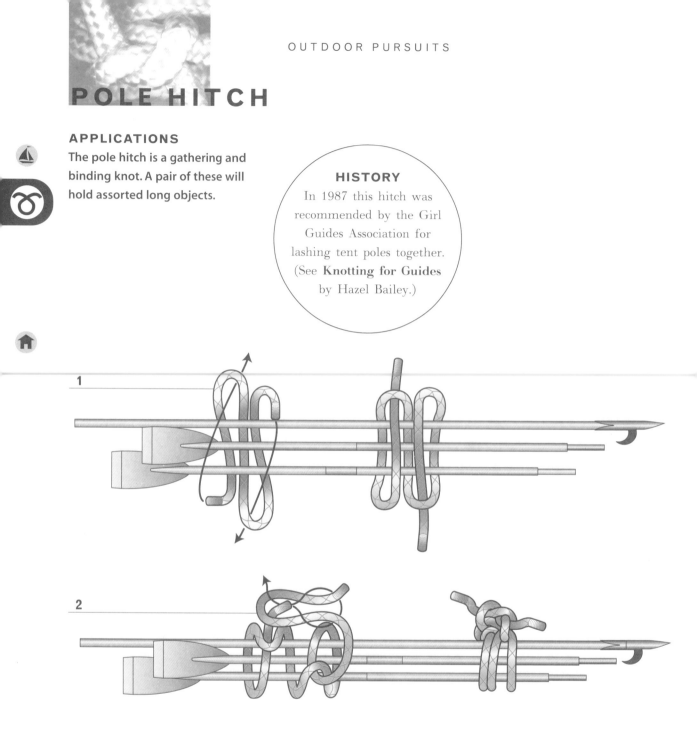

1

2

METHOD
Arrange the cord in an S- or Z-shape beneath the assembled objects, and tuck both ends through opposite bights (fig. 1). Draw tight and tie off with a reef knot (fig 2, and see p. 134).

<74>

HALF-HITCHING

APPLICATIONS

A simple way to tie long parcels, half-hitching is closely akin to marline hitching (see p. 76). Many people cannot tell the difference, but there is one. Half-hitching can be done without resort to the end of the string or cord used. (See also chain stitch lashing, p. 77.)

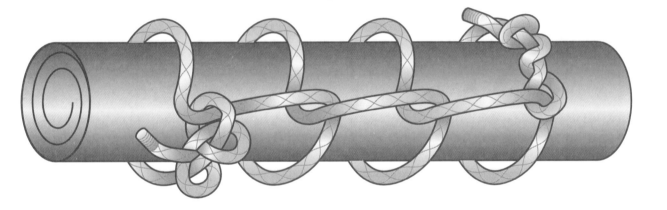

METHOD

Using a continuous line, start with a clove, rolling or timber hitch (see pp. 47, 48 and 49). Add as many hitches at suitable intervals as necessary. Either pass the working end around and through each time, or (with an inconveniently long line) simply slide underhand loops over the end of the bale or parcel as you go. Tie off as you like.

<75>

MARLINE HITCHING

APPLICATIONS

Although at first glance marline hitching is identical to half-hitching (see p. 75), there is a little more tying involved than in half-hitching, but this method of securing a parcel gives a better grip.

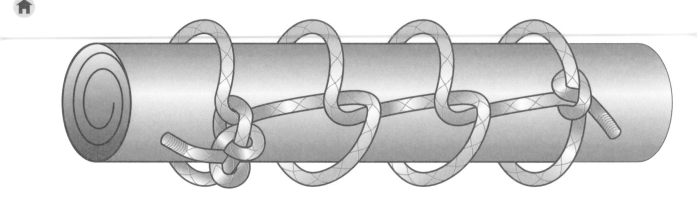

METHOD

Unlike half-hitching, which is a series of single hitches, marline hitching uses simple overhand knots tied along the length of the object(s) to be parcelled. Note that a working end is needed for marline hitching, although not for half-hitching. It is tricky to discern the subtle difference between these two techniques just by looking; but slide half-hitches off their bundle and they fall apart, whereas marline hitches end up as a series of overhand knots.

<76>

CHAIN STITCH LASHING

APPLICATIONS

This technique is ideal for securing a range of soft and awkward long bundles, from rolled carpets to furled sails. There is give and take in the embrace of the lashing, and it is therefore suitable for loads that bend and flex.

METHOD

This technique needs a long rope or cord. Start with a timber hitch (fig. 1, and see p. 47). Loop one bight through the other, finishing off with a clove hitch (figs 2–3, and see p. 48). Untie the clove hitch, withdraw the end, pull and watch it unravel.

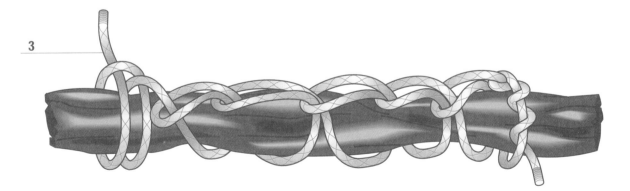

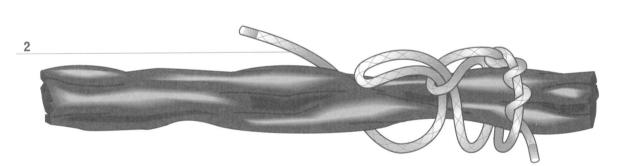

<77>

TRUCKER'S HITCH

APPLICATIONS
This hitch gives tension to the lashing on a loaded vehicle. (See also diamond hitch, p. 79.)

METHOD
Treble the rope parts in your hand and hook an overhand loop onto the uppermost bight (fig. 1). A trade trick is to put one or two twists into the long bight (fig. 2) before doing anything else, to prevent the knot from spilling as you pull it taut and take up the slack (known as swigging). Now pull a bight of the free line through the twisted bight, pass it around a convenient anchorage, and pull (fig. 3). Lead the line around the next anchorage point and repeat the process.

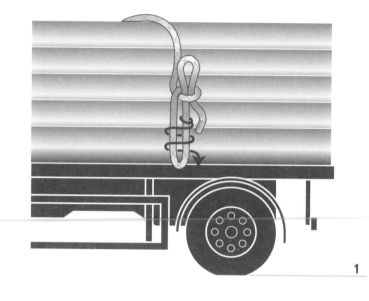

1

HISTORY
The other name for this contrivance is the waggoner's hitch, which implies that it is as old as carts and carriages. The first part of the knot (fig. 1) is the bell-ringer's knot, described as early as 1815.

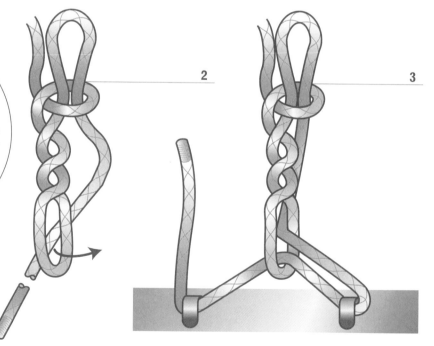

2

3

<78>

DIAMOND HITCH

APPLICATIONS

This hitch secures loads to pack animals or to off-road and other vehicles. (See also trucker's hitch, p. 78.)

METHOD

Pass a continuous line around six anchorage points (figs 1–3). The characteristic feature of this hitch is the twisted middle parts, which allow the slack to be taken up where necessary as the load shifts and strains.

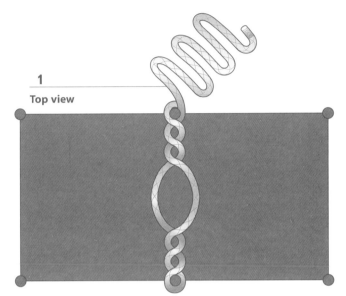

1
Top view

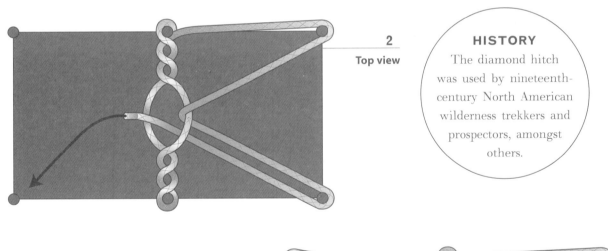

2
Top view

HISTORY

The diamond hitch was used by nineteenth-century North American wilderness trekkers and prospectors, amongst others.

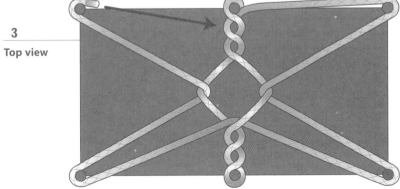

3
Top view

<79>

JUG, JAR OR BOTTLE SLING

APPLICATIONS

With its two cord handles extending from an interwoven collar, this sling will grip the neck of almost any container. The knot parts exert a ratchet action, tightening the sling so that it is unlikely to work loose. The jug sling was used by cowboys to improvise a hackamore or emergency horse bridle.

1

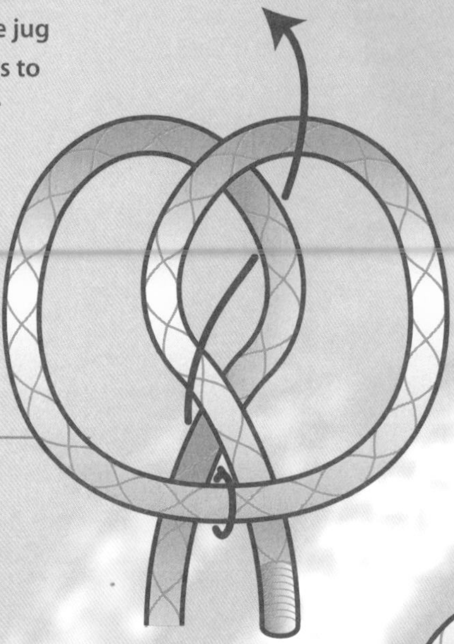

2

3

4

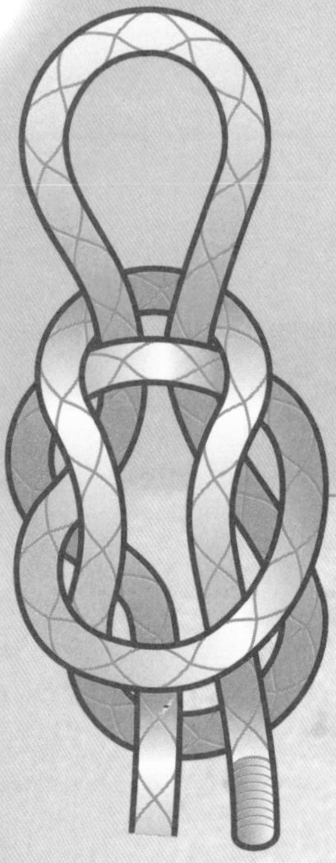

<80>

METHOD

There are several ways to tie this complex knot, only one of which is shown (figs 1–4). Don't try to make the long loops equal; just tie the two ends through the existing loop with a fisherman's knot (see p. 39) and you will have a pair of self-adjusting handles (fig. 5). A more ingenious solution is Asher's Equalizer (figs 6–7).

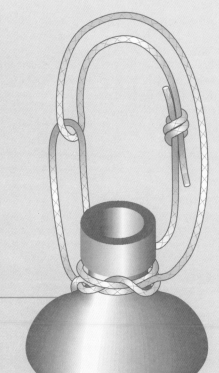

5

6

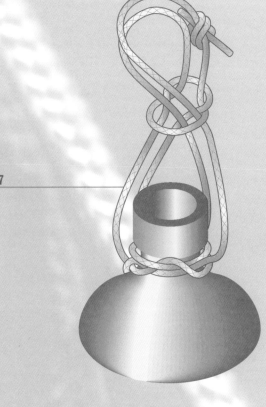

7

HISTORY

In the first century AD, an obscure Greek physician named Heraklas described this contrivance as a surgical sling. Johann Röding, author of **Allgemeines Wörterbuch der Marine** (1795), called it a jug sling, and E.N. Little referred to it as a jar sling knot in his **Log Book Notes** (1889). Asher's Equalizers (figs 5–7) were invented in the mid-1980s by Harry Asher.

<81>

caving and climbing

FROST KNOT

APPLICATIONS
This knot is used to make the steps or rungs in the short, improvised webbing or tape ladders known as étriers (from the French for stirrup).

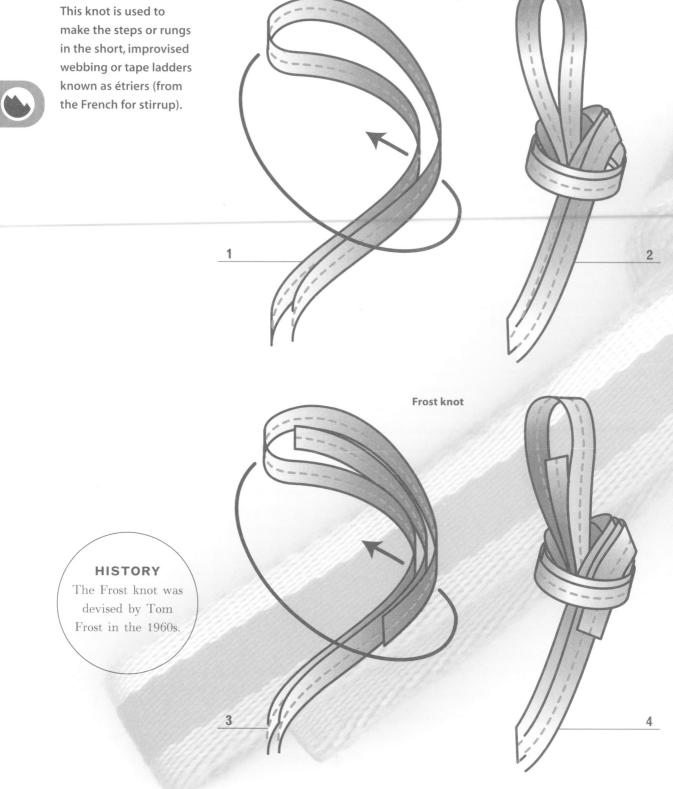

Overhand loop knot

1

2

Frost knot

3

4

<84>

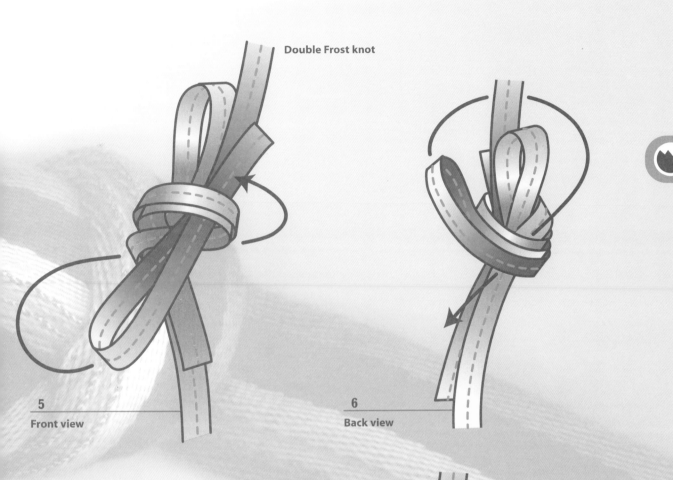

Double Frost knot

5
Front view

6
Back view

7

METHOD

This is like an overhand loop knot (figs 1–2) but incorporates both webbing parts and ends in the completed knot (figs 3–4). Like the double Frost knot (figs 5–7), it is related to the tape knot (see p. 100).

<85>

ALPINE BUTTERFLY

APPLICATIONS

This fixed loop is tied in the bight of a rope and is clipped into by the middle climber in a team of three. It can be pulled in two (or even three) directions at once without distorting or capsizing. It can also permit the temporary use of a damaged rope, by isolating a flawed section within the loop.

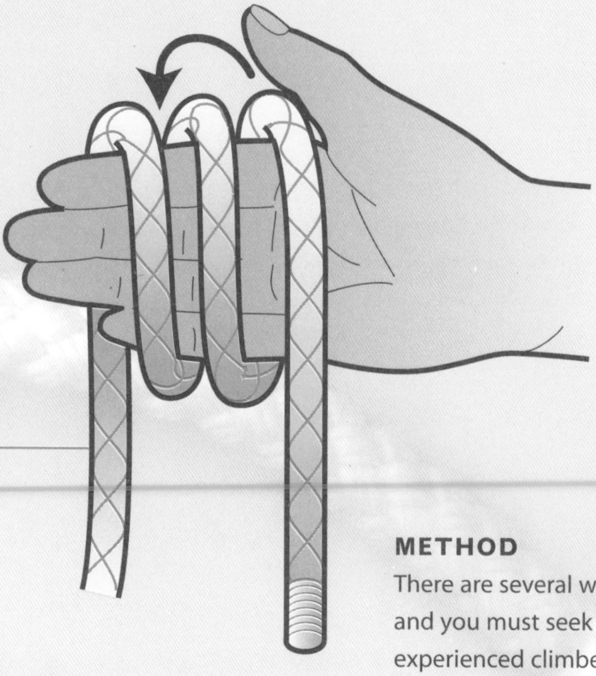

1

METHOD

There are several ways to tie this knot and you must seek the guidance of experienced climbers whichever you use. The method shown here (figs 1–6) is possibly the easiest to learn.

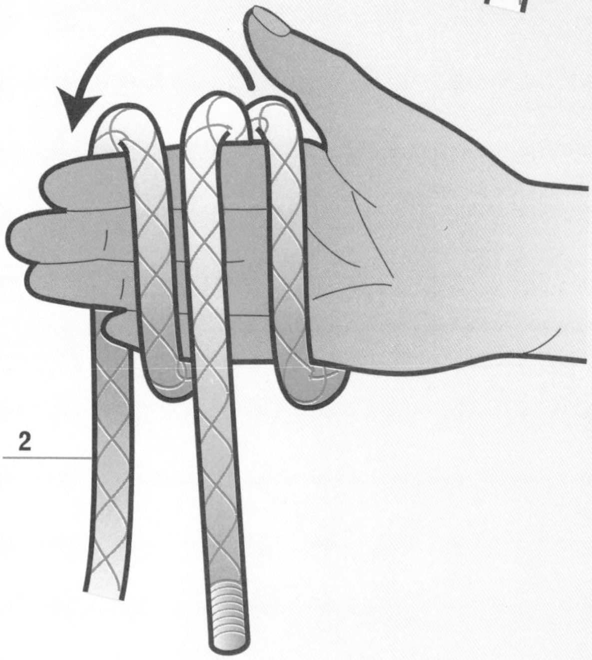

2

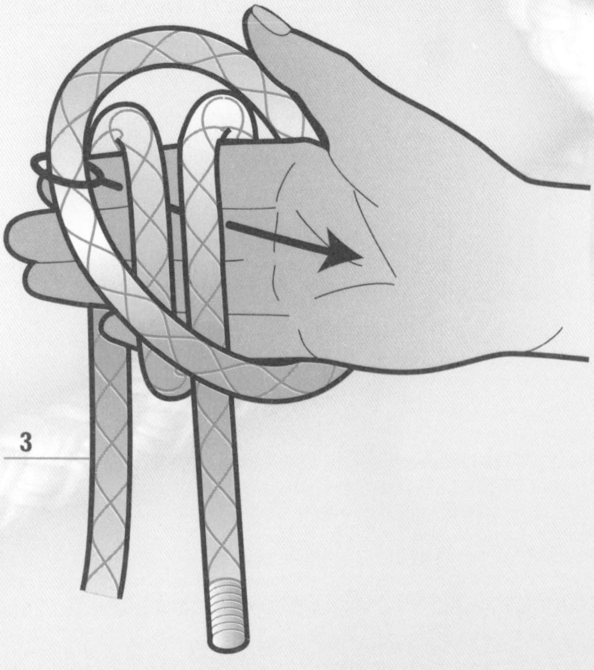

3

<86>

5

4

6

<87>

FIGURE EIGHT LOOPS

APPLICATIONS

For tying into the rope, anchoring non-climbers, or any other purpose for which a single, double or triple loop knot is required, the figure eight knot layout is a versatile alternative to a bowline, a bowline in the bight or a triple bowline (see pp. 36, 38 and 92).

1

2

METHOD

Tie directly in the bight (figs 1–4) for a single loop knot. Remove any twists so that paired parts of the knot are parallel with one another. For maximum strength, climbers recommend that the standing bight – marked X in fig. 3 – should lie on the outside of the bend, with the working-end bight on the inside. Secure the working end with an overhand knot to the standing part (figs 5–6), or tuck it back through the knot (fig. 7). This knot uses 1.2 metres (4 ft) of 9-mm ($^3/_{10}$-in) rope and 1.5 metres (5 ft) of 11-mm ($^2/_5$-in) rope.

3

<88>

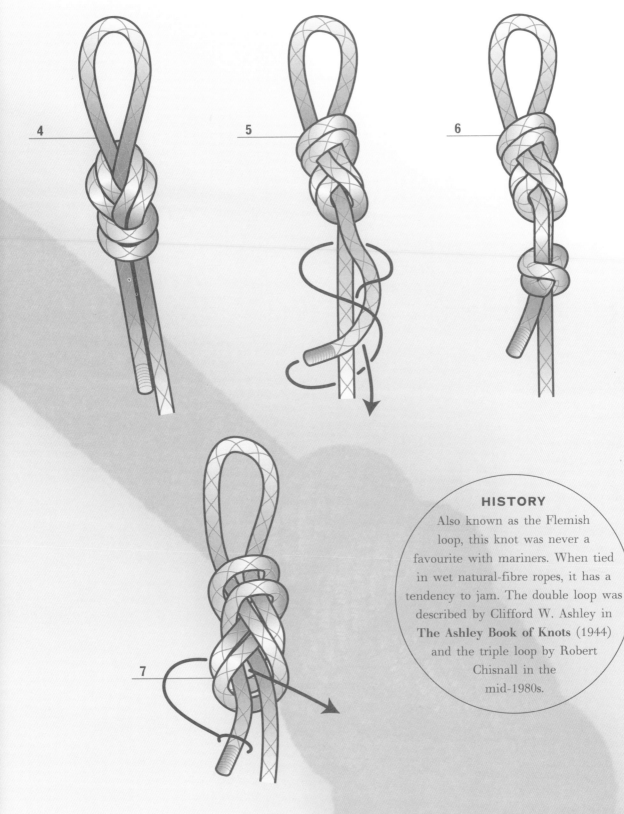

4

5

6

7

HISTORY

Also known as the Flemish loop, this knot was never a favourite with mariners. When tied in wet natural-fibre ropes, it has a tendency to jam. The double loop was described by Clifford W. Ashley in **The Ashley Book of Knots** (1944) and the triple loop by Robert Chisnall in the mid-1980s.

<89>

FIGURE EIGHT LOOPS (cont'd)

METHOD (cont'd)
Both double loop (figs 1–4) and triple loop (figs 5–8) variants of this knot may be conveniently tied in the bight.

Double figure eight loop

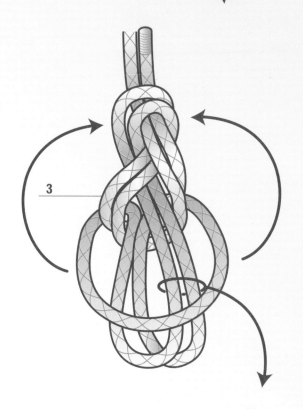
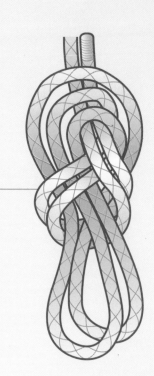

<90>

Triple figure eight loop

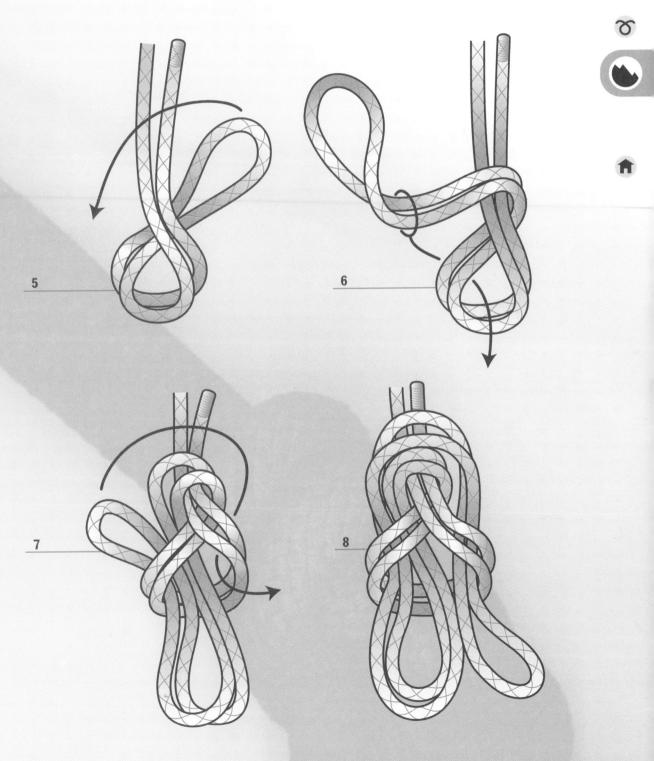

5

6

7

8

<91>

TRIPLE BOWLINE

APPLICATIONS

The triple bowline can be used to make a sit sling, chest sling or full harness. The loops must be painstakingly adjusted to fit the appropriate parts of the body.

METHOD

Tie a bowline in a doubled bight of rope (figs 1–4). Adjusting the first two loops and accommodating the slack in the final one is fiddly to do but not hard to figure out.

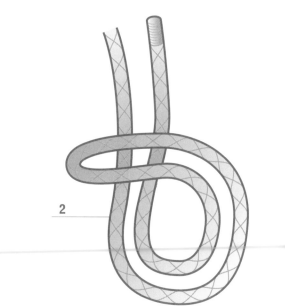

1

2

3

4

HISTORY

This knot seems to have emerged in print only in recent decades.

<92>

TRIPLE BOWLINE VARIATION

APPLICATIONS

This variation is useful for training purposes, when it can be used for belaying to a fixed anchorage (e.g., a tree). It has a loop plus two lines to which an instructor and pupil can be attached.

METHOD

Tie a triple bowline in the doubled rope (figs 1–2) and tuck the working bight back through to create a figure eight layout in the completed knot (fig. 3).

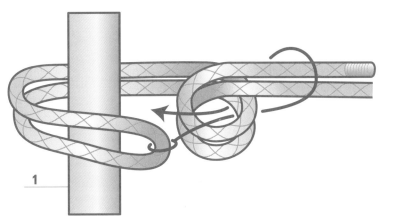

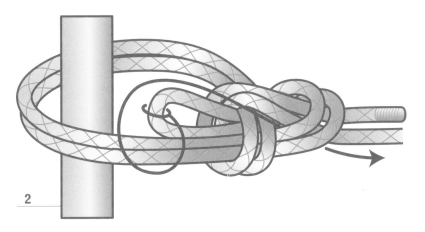

HISTORY

The triple bowline shown here was devised by Robert Chisnall in the mid-1980s.

<93>

TRIDENT LOOP

APPLICATIONS

This is a newcomer in the knot world. It was cautiously proposed by its inventor (see below) as an alternative to the figure eight loop (see p. 88). Initial tests indicate it to have a breaking strength of about 70%, stronger than the common bowline (60%) and weaker than the figure eight loop (80%). Given the tensile strength of modern climbing ropes, its middle ranking may be less significant than its security – shock-load test results show no slippage (not even a millimetre).

METHOD

First form an overhand knot (fig. 1). Next tuck a bight (fig. 2). Finally, pass the working end through the bight and add an extra half-hitch (figs 3–4).

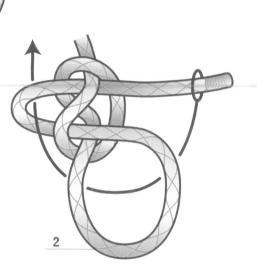

1

2

3

4

HISTORY

Sound bends often make good loop knots (the opposite applies, too) and Robert M. Wolfe, MD, of Chicago based this knot on Clifford W. Ashley's bend no. 1452 in **The Ashley Book of Knots**. Dr Wolfe sent me a detailed report on the trident loop in 1995.

<94>

ADJUSTABLE LOOP AND BEND

APPLICATIONS

This practical slide-and-grip knot can be grasped and shifted easily by hand in either direction but locks up firmly under load. After the load is removed, the knot may be slid along the rope again. The momentum of a fall will cause the knot to slide and so absorb energy. The slippage load is predictable and can be controlled to some extent, any variation being due to inconsistent tying.

Tests on this knot produced the following data: in 2.5-cm (1-in) tape, four round turns were at least 25% stronger than three turns, while in 7–8-mm ($\frac{1}{3}$-in) cord, four round turns were about 10% stronger than three turns. These are provisional figures based upon some inconclusive test results. Later tests involving 5.5-mm ($\frac{1}{4}$-in) Kevlar indicated that, when used as adjustable **bends**, these knots grip (i.e., do not slip) and break at around 80% of the absolute rupture load of the material used. This figure may be an underestimate.

HISTORY

This knot was devised in 1982 by Canadian mountain and building climber Robert Chisnall.

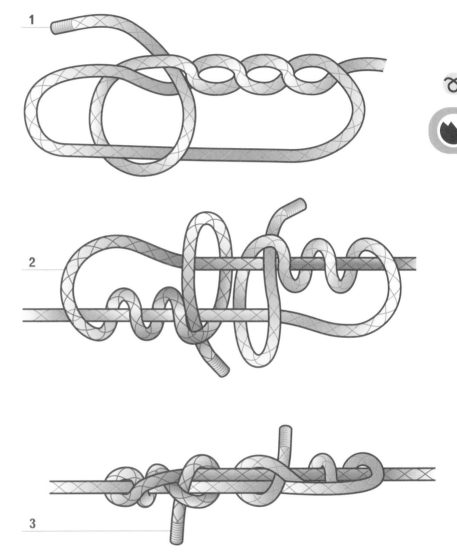

METHOD

Use rope or webbing (tape). Tie the knot neatly and snugly (fig. 1). The tape ends should be left at least 8 cm (3 in) long. For real belt-and-braces peace of mind, add an overhand knot to each end, or turn the ends back on themselves and sew them in place to form bulky tabs. Two of these knots form an endless sling (figs 2–3). If the two knots are kept apart, each acts as its own Prusik (see p. 104) – should one knot fail, the second serves as a back-up; if both slip, they merely come together and hold like a fisherman's knot (see p. 39).

<95>

FLEMISH BEND

APPLICATIONS
The Flemish bend joins
two climbing ropes.

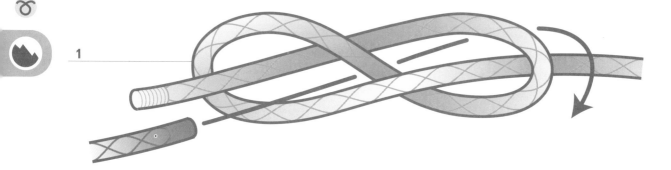

1

2

X

Y

METHOD
Make a figure eight knot in one line, then tie the other
working end parallel with it (fig. 1). As with the figure
eight loop, the standing bights (marked X and Y in fig.
2) should lie on the outside of the knot in each
instance, with the working-end bights on the inside.

<96>

OVERHAND SHORTENING

APPLICATIONS
This knot makes two fixed and secure leg loops for a harness.

HISTORY
The overhand shortening was first shown to me by the mountaineer Robert Chisnall in the early 1990s.

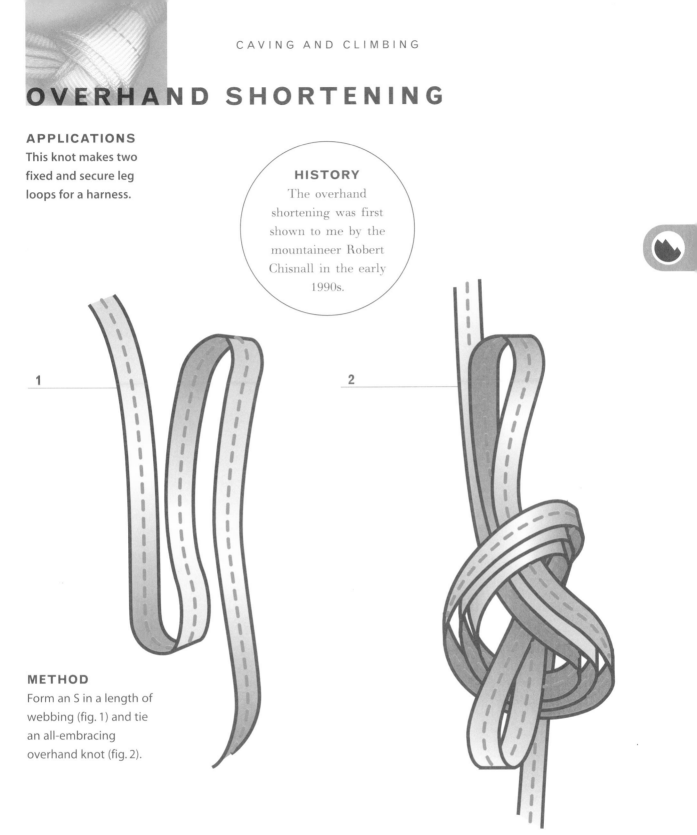

1

2

METHOD
Form an S in a length of webbing (fig. 1) and tie an all-embracing overhand knot (fig. 2).

<97>

DOUBLE AND TRIPLE FISHERMAN'S KNOT

APPLICATIONS
Use these strengthened knots to secure two ropes together and to make endless slings.

Double fisherman's knot

1

2

3

METHOD
Make two parallel, sliding double overhand knots (figs 1–3). For slippery cord and conditions, triple overhand knots may be preferred (figs 4–6). Leave generous ends 7–8 cm (3 in) long, and tape them to their adjacent standing parts. The knot will take 75 cm (2½ ft) of 9-mm (³⁄₁₀-in) rope and over 1 metre (3½ ft) of 11-mm (²⁄₅-in) rope.

<98>

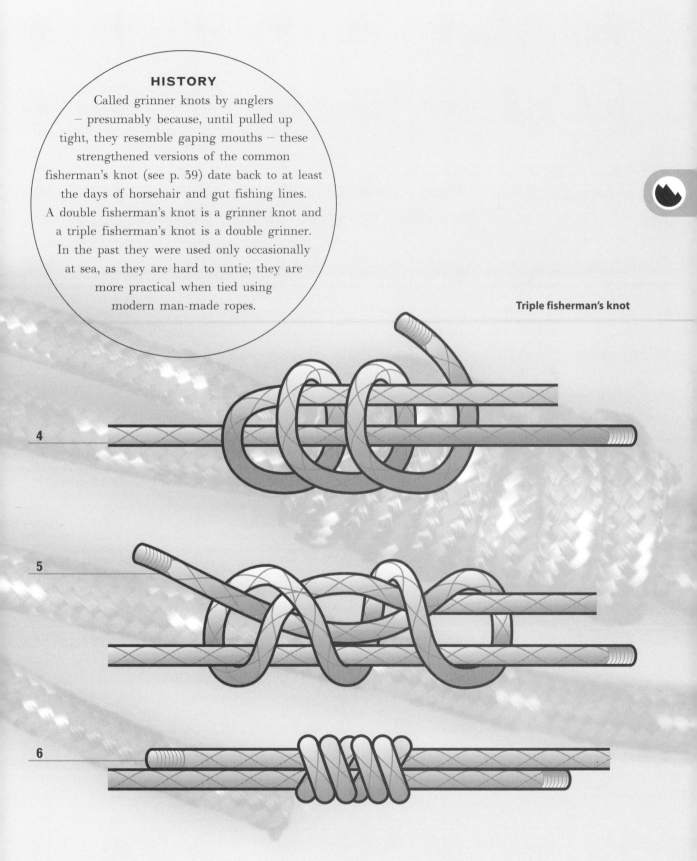

HISTORY

Called grinner knots by anglers – presumably because, until pulled up tight, they resemble gaping mouths – these strengthened versions of the common fisherman's knot (see p. 39) date back to at least the days of horsehair and gut fishing lines. A double fisherman's knot is a grinner knot and a triple fisherman's knot is a double grinner. In the past they were used only occasionally at sea, as they are hard to untie; they are more practical when tied using modern man-made ropes.

Triple fisherman's knot

4

5

6

<99>

TAPE KNOT

APPLICATIONS

This is the bend recommended for climbers' tape or webbing. It also works in rope, cord, string and the finest monofilaments. It can be used to form endless loops or slings.

1

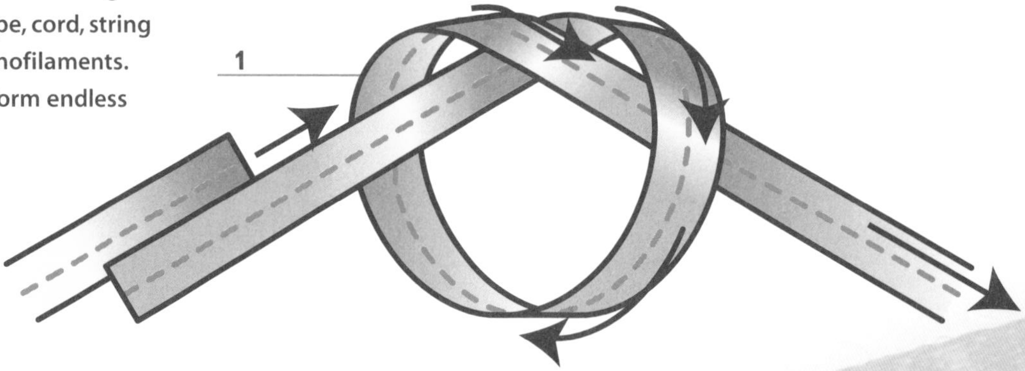

2

HISTORY

In **The Compleat Angler**, the classic work on fishing first published in 1653, Isaak Walton called this knot the water knot. Hutton referred to it as the ring knot in his **Dictionary** of 1815. In 1919 Dr Holden, author of **Streamcraft**, reverted to the name 'water knot'. The water/ring knot has also been known as the gut knot. In addition, the water knot is another name for the fisherman's knot; for this reason, the name 'tape knot' – used by modern climbers – has been adopted here.

<100>

METHOD

In anything up to a couple of metres (6 ft) long, just lay the two lengths parallel and together, then tie an overhand knot in both at once. Remove unwanted twists before pulling tight. In longer stuff, tie the overhand knot in the end of one length (fig. 1) and pass the other end through and around to mirror the first knot (fig. 2). Alternatively, tie both working ends simultaneously (fig. 3).

The tape knot is straightforward to tie using webbing, but remember to leave longish working ends, which should then be taped to their adjacent standing parts. Check the knot regularly to make sure it does not work loose. In 25-mm (1-in) tape, at least two 30-cm (1-ft) lengths will be needed for this knot.

When tying the tape knot in rope, you have a choice of two layouts. Both are secure, but one is thought to be weaker than the other. Check the completed knot. The cords must be parallel, with no cross-overs. Then, with the belly of the knot underneath, ensure that both short ends emerge on top (fig. 4). If the ends are underneath, the knot may be weakened.

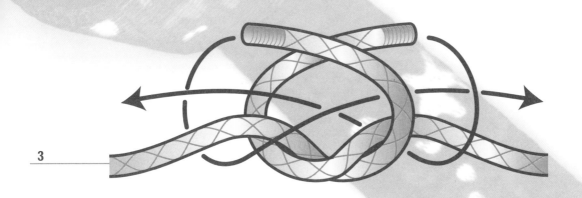

3

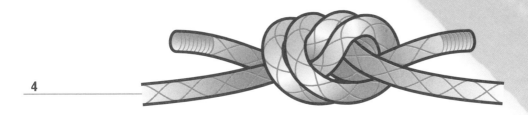

4

<101>

MUNTER FRICTION HITCH

APPLICATIONS
When tied in kernmantel rope, this is a very effective means of belaying, abseiling or absorbing the energy of a fall. It also reverses to give slack or tension as required.

Single Munter friction hitch

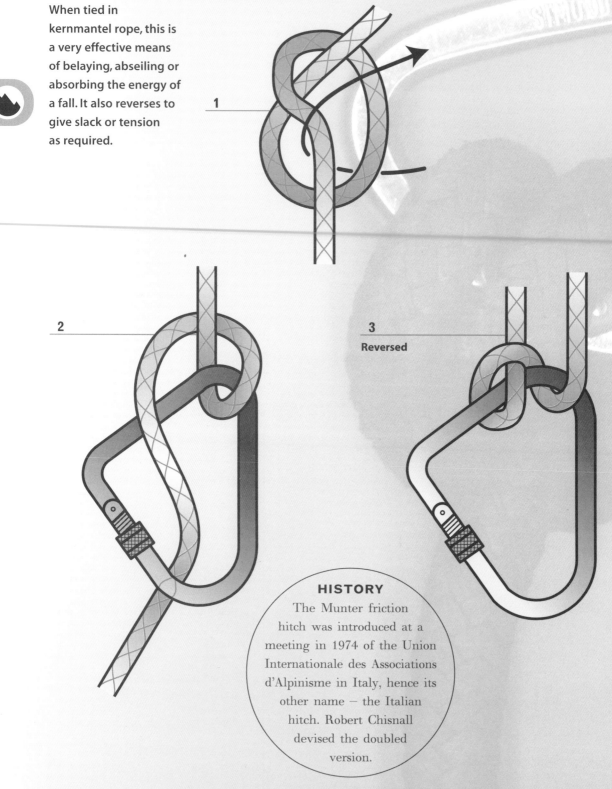

1

2

3
Reversed

HISTORY
The Munter friction hitch was introduced at a meeting in 1974 of the Union Internationale des Associations d'Alpinisme in Italy, hence its other name – the Italian hitch. Robert Chisnall devised the doubled version.

<102>

METHOD

Sheath-and-core rope should be used for this hitch, with one of the wide gate, pear-shaped karabiners now produced to accommodate it. (Laid line is not suitable.) Clip into an unfinished overhand knot (fig. 1) for the single hitch (fig. 2). This is in effect a dynamic crossing knot (see parcel ties, p. 147). Note that 9-mm ($^3/_{10}$-in) rope will take up about 30–35 cm (at least 1-ft), while 11-mm ($^2/_5$-in) rope will use 45 cm ($1^1/_2$-ft) in this hitch. When paying out rope, or taking in slack, it is normal for the configuration of this hitch to reverse (fig. 3).

For belaying with 9-mm (3/10-in) rope, which often needs more friction than 11 mm (2/5-in), use the doubled variant (figs 4–5). It too is reversible (fig. 6).

Double Munter friction hitch

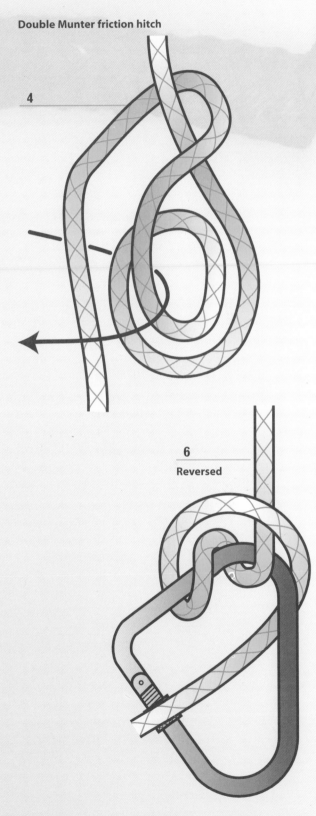

4

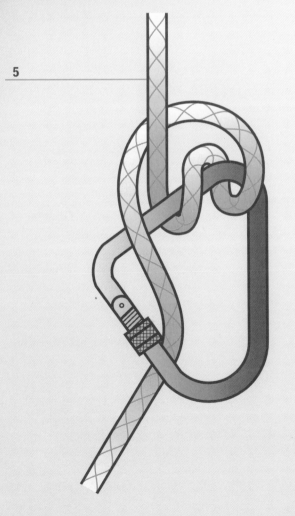

5

6
Reversed

<103>

PRUSIK KNOT

APPLICATIONS

Strictly speaking, this is not a knot but a hitch of the slide-and-grip sort, recommended for climbers faced with an emergency ascent. Two endless slings or strops are attached to the main climbing rope with Prusik knots. Both pass through a chest harness and one is attached to each foot. The climber's weight is supported by these stirrups. To extricate himself from a cave or crevasse, he removes the weight from one sling and slides its hitch up. Then he stands in the raised sling and repeats the process with the lower one. By this alternate load – unload – move process, a rope ladder is created, the nearest thing to hauling yourself up by your own bootstraps. Experts have been timed climbing 30 metres (100 ft) in just over one minute, or 120 metres (400 ft) in a little over nine minutes.

There are now several Prusik knots or hitches, varying in reliability and ease of use. None of them, however, can be easily released while jammed and fully loaded; weight must first be taken off the knot and the turns worked loose. Both hands may be needed; among climbers, this has caused not a few accidents and even the occasional fatality. A karabiner may be inserted to ease movement of the knots, although the load must still be clipped in to the bights of the slings. The Prusik may be used in abseiling or rappelling, but climbers must make sure that the knots are within reach and will not leave them hanging helplessly should they lose control.

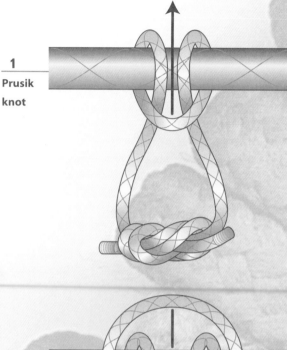

1
Prusik
knot

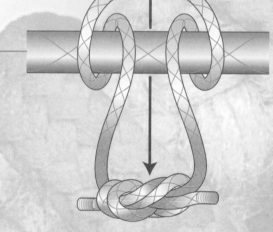

2

3

<104>

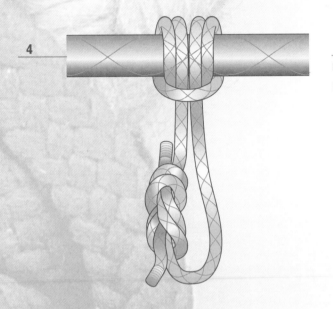

4

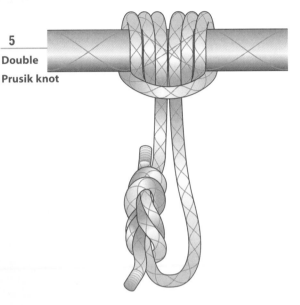

5

**Double
Prusik knot**

METHOD

Use 7-mm (¹/₄-in) accessory cord; thinner stuff will be weaker, and anything thicker will not grip as well. The cord should not be more than half the diameter of the main rope. Allow a sufficient length, as each knot alone may use at least 60 cm (2 ft) of line.

Experts disagree over whether or not there is any advantage to be gained from using rope and slings of similar composition. Softer laid or braided (i.e., more flexible) slings will grip the rope well but will be difficult to loosen and shift; in the case of harder laid or braided cord the opposite will apply. Do not use tape, for which there are other more suitable friction hitches.

A properly tied Prusik knot should hold until the sling cord breaks. If it begins to slip under load, it may continue to do so until the heat generated melts the nylon knot and it comes completely undone (quite apart from any damage done to the main climbing rope). To prevent the knot sliding – especially in icy or muddy conditions – the basic two-wrap knot (fig. 1) may have to be increased to three, a double Prusik knot (fig. 2), or even four wrapping turns.

HISTORY

An Austrian professor of music, Dr Karl Prusik, originally devised this knot during the First World War to mend the broken strings of musical instruments. In 1931 he published the instructions as a means of self-rescue for European mountaineers. The original Prusik knots were also used to safeguard a loaded rope and to attach tackle systems to raise a helpless person.

<105>

BACHMAN KNOT

APPLICATIONS

Climbers use the Bachman knot when making an ascent, often in self-rescue situations, or when hoisting a casualty with a pulley. Used with a screw-gate karabiner, it is much easier to shift than the Prusik knot (see p. 104). It works well in wet and icy ropes too.

METHOD

Use a thin karabiner and 5–6-mm ($^1\!/_4$-in) cord, which must be much thinner than the rope around which it is tied. About 55 cm (2 ft) of line will be taken up by this knot, which also works with webbing. First clip the karabiner into the sling, then wrap the line around the rope so that it spirals down and through the karabiner. If the knot slips when it's loaded, add more wrapping turns. Remember to load the sling loop, not the karabiner.

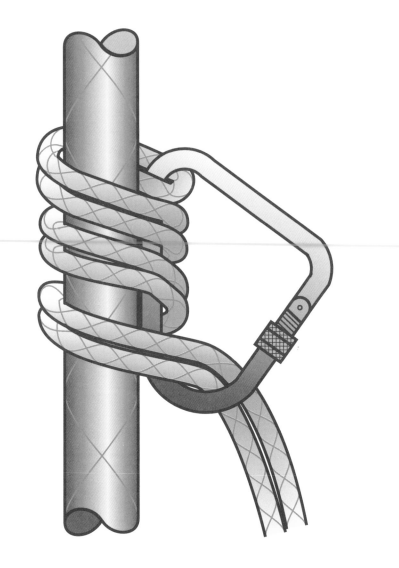

HISTORY

The Bachman knot is Austrian in origin and is the oldest of the semi-mechanical knots.

<106>

KLEMHEIST KNOT

APPLICATIONS

This is a prusiking knot for cord or webbing.

HISTORY

The origins of the Klemheist knot are unknown to me.

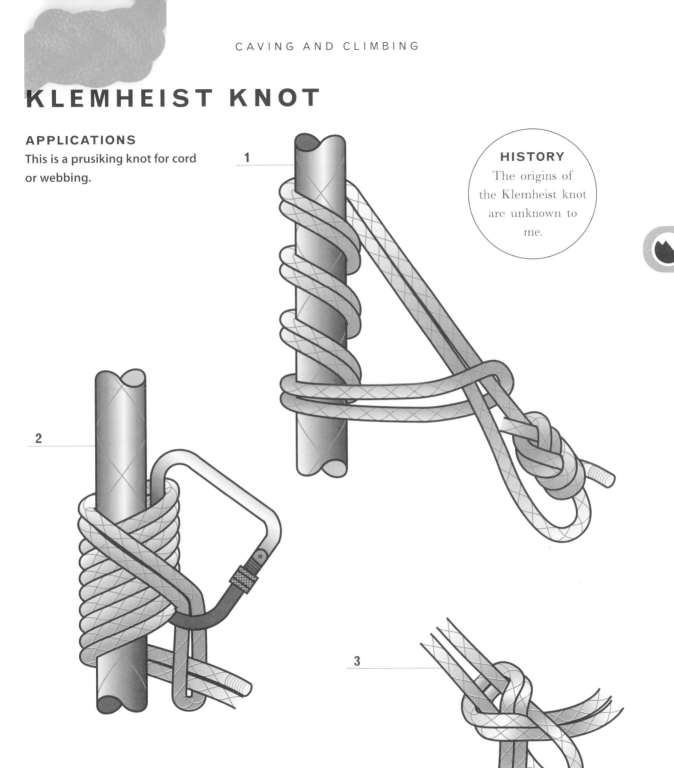

METHOD

Wrap a loop four or five times around the rope, towards the load, before passing the working loop through the standing one (fig. 1). A karabiner can be incorporated (fig. 2). Clip into the working loop where it emerges. Add more turns if the knot slips. Tying off with a sheet bend improves the Klemheist knot (fig. 3); this variation was devised by John Zwangwill.

<107>

EXTENDED FRENCH PRUSIK KNOT

APPLICATIONS

This innovative friction hitch absorbs the energy of a shock loading by sliding; it does not grip firmly until the falling load is low enough. The knot exerts friction on the enclosed rope by stretching and decreasing its diameter, so applying inward pressure and spreading the friction over a wide area.

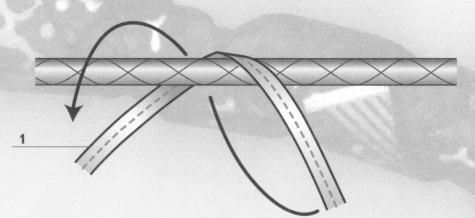

1

2

3

HISTORY

The basic French Prusik knot in cordage seems to date from the early 1960s. In 1977 Robert Thrun recommended more racking turns to extend the knot. The Chinese finger-trap version shown here is intended to be tied in tape and was created by Robert Chisnall, who described it to me in 1981.

<108>

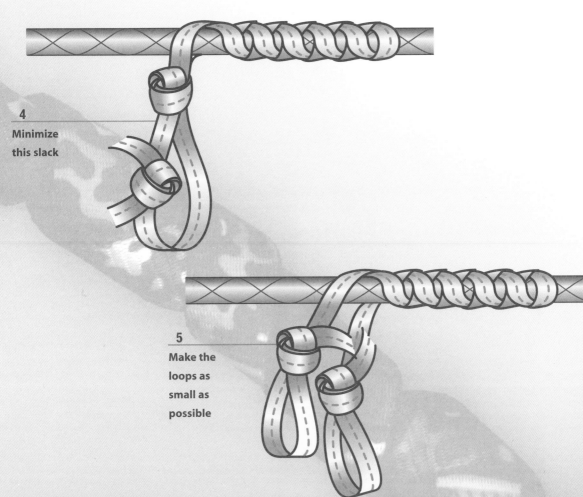

4
Minimize
this slack

5
Make the
loops as
small as
possible

METHOD

At first sight this knot looks complex, but it becomes
easy with practice. Use 25-mm (1-in) tape. (Tubular
tape is probably best.) Eight to ten racking turns are
sufficient (figs 1–3). The cross-overs must alternate, and
the window spaces must be as small as possible (i.e.,
only a little of the rope should be visible). Join the two
ends as close to the knot as possible, the tighter the
better (fig. 4). Fig. 5 shows another method using pre-
tied loops.

Illustrated here on a single rope, the French
Prusik knot works equally well on doubled abseil or
rappel lines. To release it, grasp the upper part of the
knot and tug it down to shorten the knot.

<109>

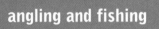

PALOMAR KNOT

APPLICATIONS

A very strong knot (95-100%) for attaching hooks, swivels, lures or sinkers, or which may be used as an arbor knot.

METHOD

Tie an overhand knot in the bight, including the hook, lure, ring or swivel (fig. 1). Then pass the loop over the attachment and tighten everything (figs 2-4).

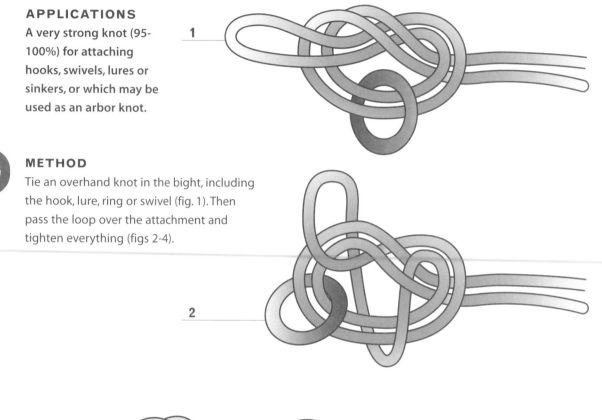

HISTORY

I have no idea, except that there is Mount Palomar in California, the site of an observatory.

<112>

JANSIK SPECIAL

APPLICATIONS
A very strong (98-100%) attachment for hook, lure or swivel.

METHOD
Pass the working end twice through the ring (figs 1-2) and then wrap three times around the three adjacent sections of line (fig. 3). Moisten the knot and pull steadily on hook, standing part and tag end at once to tighten the knot (fig. 4).

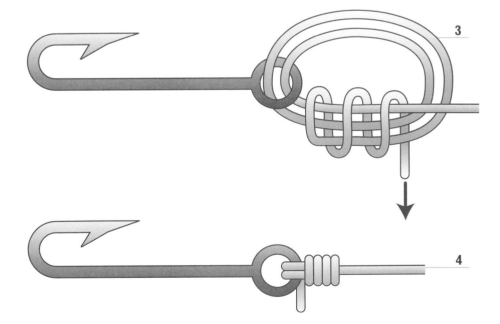

<113>

ANGLER'S LOOP KNOT

APPLICATIONS

This knot makes a relatively strong and very secure fixed loop in anything from slender monofilament to large rope.

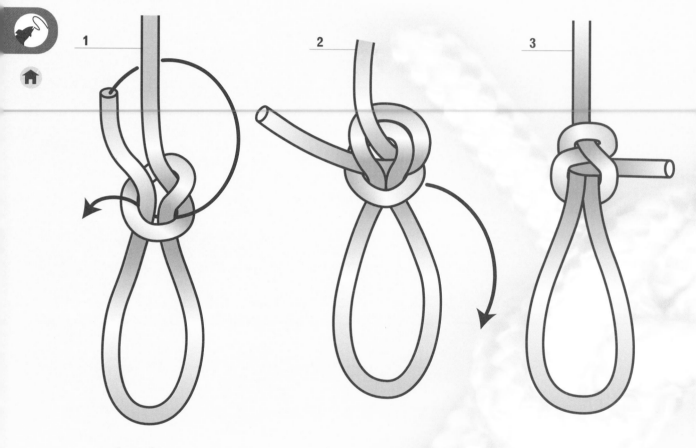

Front view

1

2

3

Back view

METHOD

To learn what this knot looks and feels like when tied correctly, tie a slipped stopper knot and then interweave the working end as shown (figs 1–3). Next, master the figure-of-eight, wrap-and-tuck approach (figs 4–6).

<114>

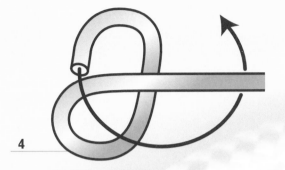

4

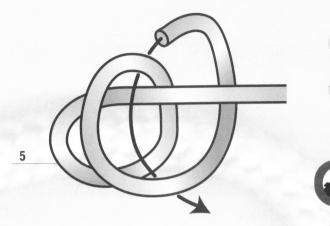

5

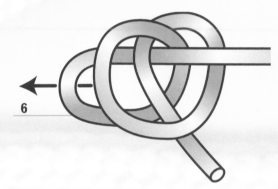

6

HISTORY

The angler's loop knot was
mentioned by Isaak Walton in **The
Compleat Angler** (1653). It was an excellent
knot for tying in fishermen's old-fashioned gut
lines – hence its other name, the perfection loop –
and survived the nylon revolution. However, seafarers
never liked it because of its tendency to jam in the old
natural-fibre ropes. It suits synthetic lines, though, and
even works in bungee (elastic shock) cord, where
other loop knots may fail. As Clifford W. Ashley
wrote in **The Ashley Book of Knots** (1944):
'Old knots long out of use have a way of
coming back into this workaday world
with renewed vigour and
usefulness.'

BLOOD LOOP DROPPER KNOT

APPLICATIONS

Some anglers say that this is a strong starting knot, and like to use it with the paternoster system of fishing tackle; others think it weakens the leader and ought to be restricted to fly-fishing. It is, nonetheless, an item in most anglers' repertoires.

METHOD

Tie a triple overhand knot and pull a bight down through it before drawing everything up tight (figs 1–3).

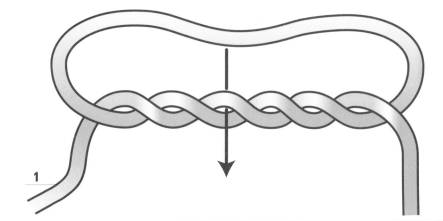

HISTORY

The idea behind this knot is an old one; often it is simply constructed from the ends of a blood knot (see p. 122) that have been overhand knotted together, or even from a separate knotted loop inserted through a tight blood knot. It is also referred to as a dropper loop.

<116>

SURGEON'S LOOP

APPLICATIONS

The surgeon's loop creates the leader loops or sea traces needed for the attachment of hooks, etc., in most kinds of line.

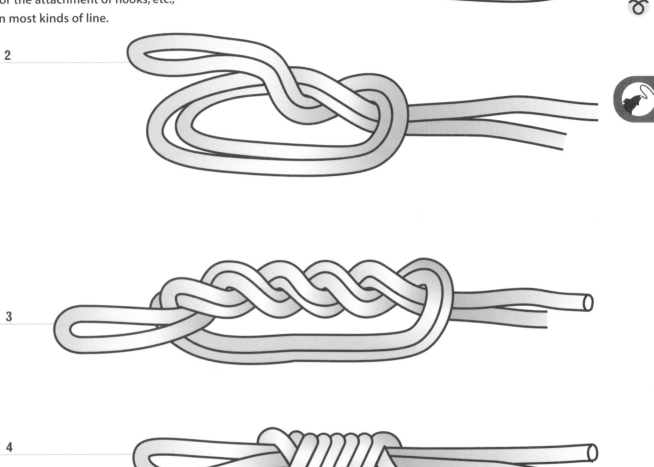

1

2

3

4

METHOD

Make a 30-cm (1-ft) bight and tie at least a triple overhand knot with the doubled line (figs 1–3). Alternatively, wrap the bight around your thumb several times, remove it and push the loop end through the resulting doughnut-shaped ring. Carefully work everything tight. Working in good light, it is possible to fair up all the turns to form a neat barrel-shape (fig. 4). In poor visibility, the surgeon's loop will be an uneven bird's nest of a knot.

HISTORY

This knot is also known as a spider hitch or thumb loop.

<117>

ARBOR KNOT

APPLICATIONS

The arbor knot attaches monofilament or braid to a reel or spool. It is also used as a shock-absorbing slide-and-grip knot when attaching a line to a hook or lure.

HISTORY
Other names for this knot are the reel knot, spool knot and Duncan loop.

METHOD

Tie as shown in figs 1–4. When pulling the knot tight, allow it to wrap around the line like a blood knot (see p. 122).

1

2

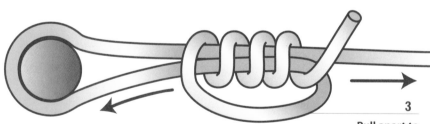

3

Pull apart to tighten knot

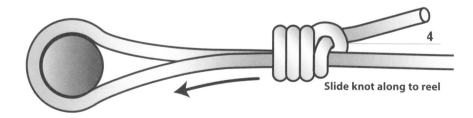

4

Slide knot along to reel

<118>

BIMINI TWIST

APPLICATIONS
This is the strongest of all loops, and is recommended for big-game fishing.

METHOD
Make a big bight, at least 1 metre (3 ft) long, and twist 20 or so turns into it (fig. 1). Place both your knees or feet into the loop and force it outwards (fig. 2), so that the initial turns ride up over themselves and then run down to form a second layer on top of the first. Once this is complete, finish off (fig. 3) with one half-hitch around a single part of the loop and a second half-hitch around both parts.

1

2
Hold firmly

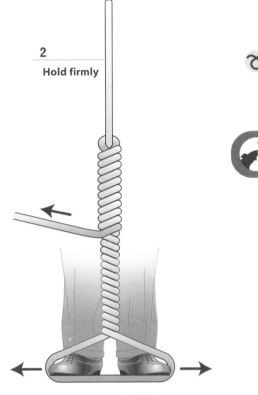

Push outwards with feet

3

HISTORY
As far as I can discover, the Bimini twist is comparatively new to knotting literature. It was described in **Practical Fishing and Boating Knots** by Lefty Kreh and Mark Sosin (1975). There is a Bimini Island in the Bahamas.

<119>

GRINNER KNOT

APPLICATIONS

The grinner knot is used
for joining lines. When
these are the same size,
it has a breaking
strength of about 75%;
in lines of unequal
diameter the breaking
strength is reduced to
about 65%.

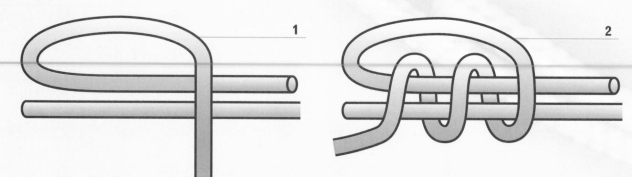

METHOD

Place the lines parallel and tie a double overhand knot (see
p. 20) with one working end around the adjacent standing part
(figs 1-3). Repeat with the other end (figs 4–5). Draw up snug
(fig. 6). When tying this knot in braided or twisted lines, it is
possible to roll and flatten it, so that it passes easily through the
guides of a rod, by first fraying both ends.

Use triple overhand knots (see p. 20) to create a double
grinner knot.

<120>

4

5

6

HISTORY

This knot is also known as the double uni-knot, the English knot and the grapevine knot. Its use in angling has been credited to the English angler Richard Walker. But Clifford W. Ashley knew it in the 1940s, describing it in **The Ashley Book of Knots**, and in fact it is no more than a version of the classic **double** fisherman's knot (see p. 98). A bloodthirsty South London boy asked me in 1981 if I knew '... the knot to cut fishes' 'eads orf.' He then mimed inserting a fish into this open knot and quickly pulling the knot shut. A double grinner or grapevine (occasionally referred to as a paragum knot) is a **triple** fisherman's knot.

<121>

BLOOD KNOT

APPLICATIONS

When this knot joins lines of the same size, it has a breaking strength of about 85%. In lines of unequal diameter, the thinner of the two lines must be used double; the knot strength then increases to around 90%. (See also half-blood knot, p. 128.)

HISTORY

W.A. Hunter, author of **Fisherman's Knots and Wrinkles** (1927), reported that this knot was first shown to him by W.D. Coggeshall many years earlier on Coggeshall's return from a visit to the US. However, in **Anglers' Knots in Gut and Nylon** (1948), Stanley Barnes gives a different account. According to Barnes, the method of construction was finally worked out by Jock Purvis, a White Star liner engineer, using a microscope and cut sections of knots cast in paraffin wax. Purvis told A.H. Chaytor, who publicized what had until then been a trade secret in his book **Letters to a Salmon Fisher's Son** (1910). The blood knot is also known as the barrel knot.

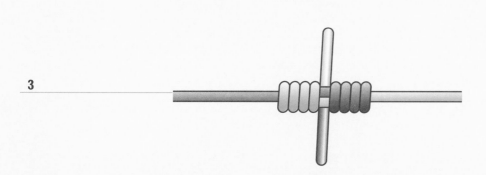

1

Outward coil

2

3

<122>

4
Inward coil

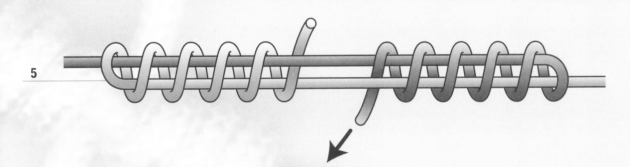

5

METHOD

Place the lines parallel and together. Wind one working end around the adjacent standing part at least five times, then bring the end back and tuck it between the two standing parts (fig. 1). Repeat, going the other way with the other end (fig. 2). Pull up snug (fig. 3).

By doubling up a very thin line, so that it is the same thickness as the one to which it is to be joined, it is possible to make what is referred to as an improved blood knot. In this case, the number of turns in the thinner line should be reduced, otherwise there will be twice as many as in the thicker one, and that is not necessary. (Although it may be difficult at first to work out the number of reductions, this can be done by trial and error.)

Outward-coiled knots must be allowed to wrap around the line as they tighten. On an inward-coiled knot (figs 4–5), the turns are made that way, and so this version may be preferred.

<123>

LINFIT KNOT

APPLICATIONS

An alternative to the grinner knot (see p. 120), this is best suited to thick, hard and springy lines.

METHOD

Long working ends should be left when tying this knot (figs 1–3), as there will be a lot of slippage when it comes to be tightened. Once it is snugged up (fig. 4), this symmetrical arrangement is strong and secure.

HISTORY

Owen K. Nuttall of West Yorkshire, England, was the inventor of this knot, which he described in **Knotting Matters** in April 1993.

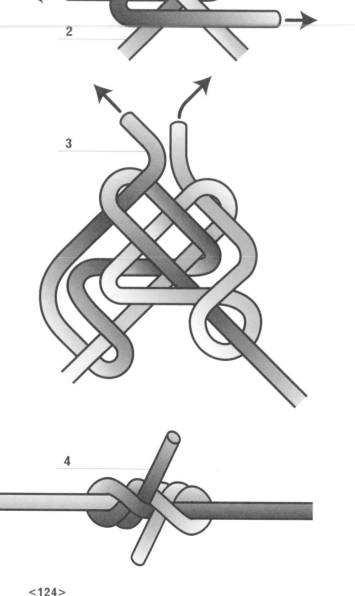

<124>

ALBRIGHT KNOT

APPLICATIONS
This knot joins lines of different size – for example, monofilament to braid, or braid to wire.

METHOD
Make a bight in the thicker of the two lines. Insert and wrap the thinner one around towards the end of the bight (figs 1–2). Finally, tuck the working end (fig. 3). Systematically work everything tight (fig. 4). (See also seizing bend, p. 42.)

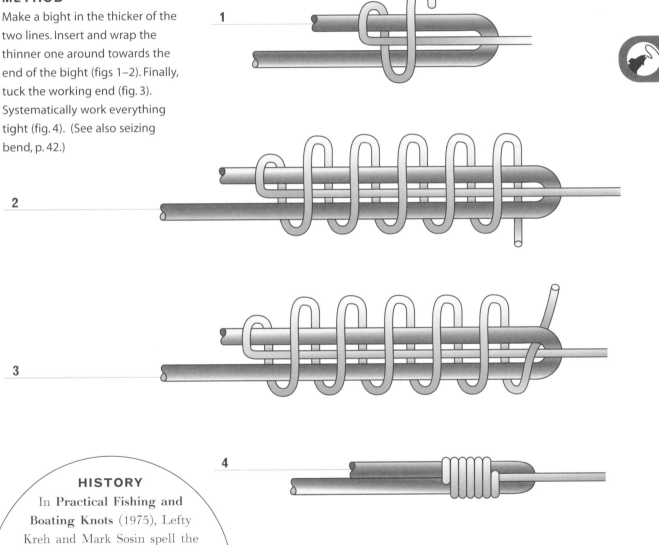

HISTORY
In **Practical Fishing and Boating Knots** (1975), Lefty Kreh and Mark Sosin spell the name of this knot Albright, but Alan B. Vare in **The Hardy Book of Fisherman's Knots** (1987) spells it Allbright. I regret I do not know which is right. The knot is also known as the Albright (or Allbright) Special.

<125>

SPADE END KNOT

APPLICATIONS

Anglers use this knot when they want to attach monofilaments to spade-ended hooks.

METHOD

Each and every wrapping turn in this knot is made by passing the loop over the point of the hook, to trap and grip both the standing part and the working end of the line (figs 1–3). This can create a lot of tension and twist in the loop, making it difficult to pull the knot tight. However, it is possible to insert counter-twist beforehand, which unwinds as the knot builds up. The completed knot (fig. 4) is in effect a whipping, and the knot may be done with a needle like a whipping (see p. 22).

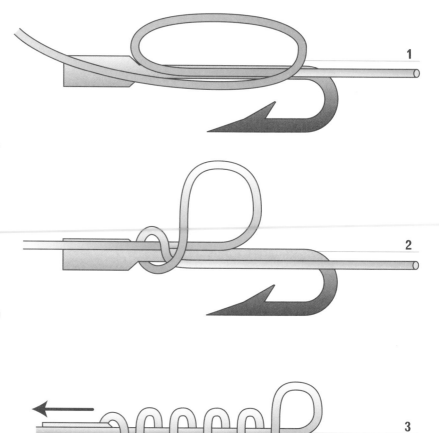

1

2

3

Pull to remove. Slack and tighten knot

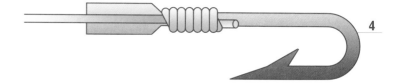

4

<126>

SNELLING

APPLICATIONS
This technique is used mainly at sea for attaching a line to eyed hooks.

METHOD
First thread the working end through the eye of the hook (fig. 1). Make a loop, hold it against the shank and wrap five or six turns around both (fig. 2). Pull on the standing end to tighten the knot, working up the rest of the parts with your fingers (fig. 3).

HISTORY
The word 'snelling' seems to have been used originally by professional long-liners, fishermen who worked with a large number of anchored and connected baited hooks. It has now been adopted by sports (mainly sea) fishermen.

1

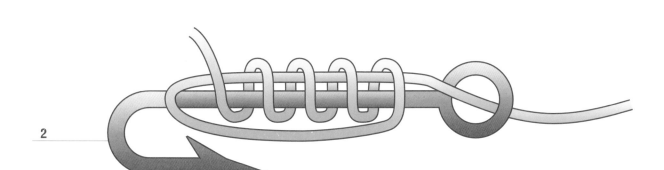

2

3

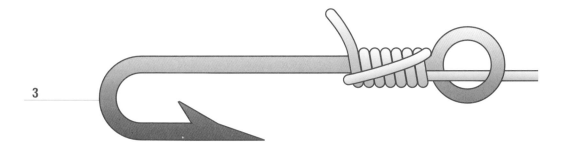

<127>

HALF-BLOOD KNOT

APPLICATIONS

The half-blood knot attaches
a line to a hook, swivel or lure.
(See also blood knot, p. 122.)

METHOD

Pass the tag end through the eye
of the hook. Wind the working end
around the standing part at least
five times and tie one half of a
blood knot (figs 1–2).

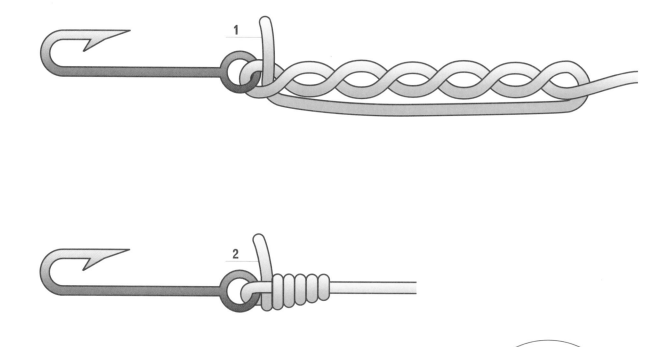

HISTORY
This knot was
developed from the
blood knot early in
the twentieth
century.

TURLE KNOT

APPLICATIONS

Unsuitable for straight-eyed hooks, this specialized knot attaches the leader to off-set eyed flies (down or up), for a straight pull.

METHOD

To tie a basic Turle knot, pass the tag end through the eye and loop it around the shank of the hook, finishing off with an overhand knot (fig. 1). Double the overhand knot for an improved Turle knot (fig. 2). Use a round turn for a double Turle knot (figs 3–4).

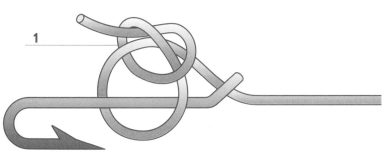

HISTORY

The Turle knot was published as early as 1841. It was made popular around 1884 in England by Major Turle of Newton Stacey, Hants, although he never claimed to have invented it. It was strongly recommended by angling writers of the day. Quite recently, this knot was wrongly referred to in print as the turtle knot.

<129>

TRUE LOVER'S KNOT

APPLICATIONS

A relatively weak knot (50–70%), the true lover's knot is tied in monofilament, or braided plastic-coated wire, to attach a lure. The small fixed loop allows the lure to move realistically.

METHOD

Pass the tag end through the eye or ring of the lure and tie a slip knot (fig. 1). Pull on the tag end to shrink the loop as necessary, then tie off onto the standing part with an identical overhand knot close to the first knot (fig. 2). Pull carefully on the lure and the standing part of the line to bed the two knots together (fig. 3).

HISTORY

Also known as the Englishman's loop knot and the Homer Rhodes knot, this is another of the knots recorded by the Greek physician Heraklas in the first century AD as a surgical sling. (See also jug, jar or bottle sling, p. 80.)

1

2

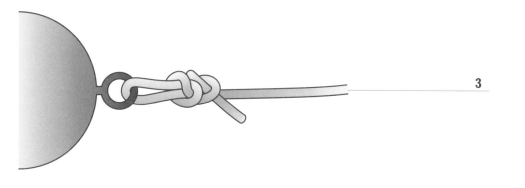

3

<130>

OFFSHORE KNOT

APPLICATIONS

The offshore knot attaches swivels or other metal loops to a long loop.

METHOD

Pass the end of the loop through the ring and bring it back down to lie on top of the two standing parts of the line. Spread out the loop and the two standing parts, then rotate the swivel or other metal attachment at least six times, so that it passes through the space marked X in fig. 1. Pull on the swivel and doubled line to tighten (fig. 2), allowing twin columns of turns to accumulate (fig. 3).

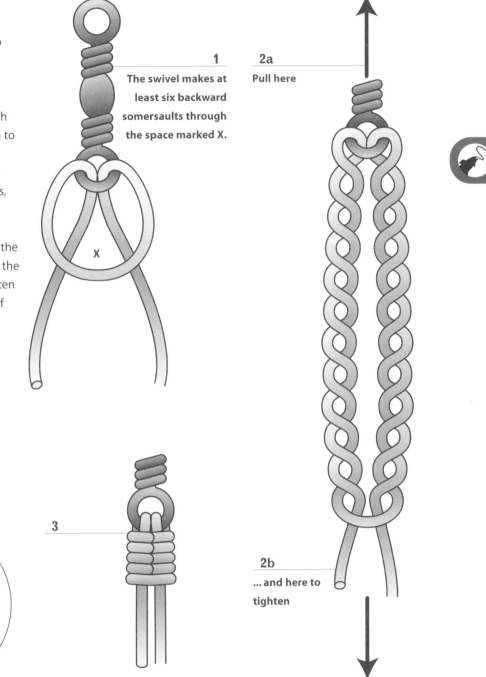

1
The swivel makes at least six backward somersaults through the space marked X.

X

2a
Pull here

2b
... and here to tighten

3

HISTORY

Another angling alias, this is really the cat's paw (see p. 146), which can be traced back to the Ancient Greeks.

<131>

REEF KNOT (SQUARE KNOT)

APPLICATIONS

Use this knot only as a binding knot, to tie together two ends of the same piece of string or other small stuff, e.g., bandages or shoelaces (with double draw-loops). Tying a reef knot around something ensures that the more strain placed upon it, the tighter it is pulled. It is not a bend and is quite weak (reducing the breaking strength of whatever it is tied in to no more than 45%), so avoid using it for ropes or any two bits of mismatched cordage. As craftsman Stuart Grainger, an ex-Master Mariner, wrote in 1985:

Reefing a sail or tying a parcel,
A reef knot the role will fulfil.
But joining two ends one should only use bends,
And a reef knot's a sure way to kill.

METHOD

'Left over right, then right over left' (figs 1-2) is the time-honoured instruction for arriving at a reef knot, avoiding the unreliable granny knot (fig. 3). Reverse these directions if a mirror image of this knot comes more naturally to you. To undo a reef knot it is sometimes possible to break it into a lark's head knot and then slide one part off the other (figs 4–5).

A reef knot may be given added security by half-hitching each working end to the standing part (fig. 6). Centre-tucking is a trifle trickier but results in a flat, semi-permanent ornamental version of the knot (fig. 7-8).

1

2

3
Granny knot

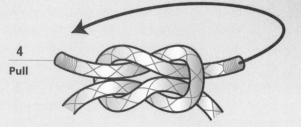

4
Pull

<134>

Slide

5

Lark's head knot

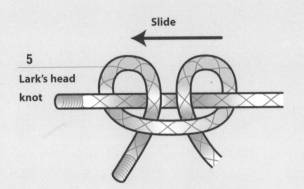

6

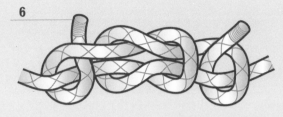

7

8

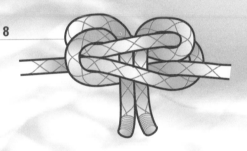

HISTORY

Neolithic man probably used the reef knot. The Ancient Greeks, Romans and Egyptians all knew this knot and were aware of its superiority over the unreliable granny knot, which both slips and jams. The Romans called it the Hercules knot, and Roman brides tied their belts with it in the hope that it would make them fertile (Hercules reputedly fathered 70 children). The Roman scientist and historian Pliny the Elder (AD 23-79) also wrote in his **Natural History** that wounds bound with this knot healed quickly. Today, first-aid instructors still teach the reef knot to tie bandages and slings, although most are unaware of the reason for doing so.

<135>

CONSTRICTOR KNOT

APPLICATIONS

This is the best of all binding knots. Use it as a temporary or semi-permanent whipping or seizing on ropes' ends; to reinforce garden trellises weakened by weather or the weight of climbing plants; to clamp hose-pipe joints; to hold glued bits and pieces together while they dry; and for a hundred other odd jobs. A double constrictor knot will fix string loops to tool and utensil handles so that they may be hung up in the garage or garden shed. (See also strangle knot, p. 142.)

METHOD

Wrap and tuck the working end (figs 1-2) and cut both ends off as short as you like (fig. 3) – this knot is not about to come undone. When the end of the object to be seized is accessible, the knot can be tied in the bight (figs 4–6). For extra-tough jobs, use a double constrictor knot (fig 7). Alternatively, apply two single constrictors alongside one another.

1

2

3

<136>

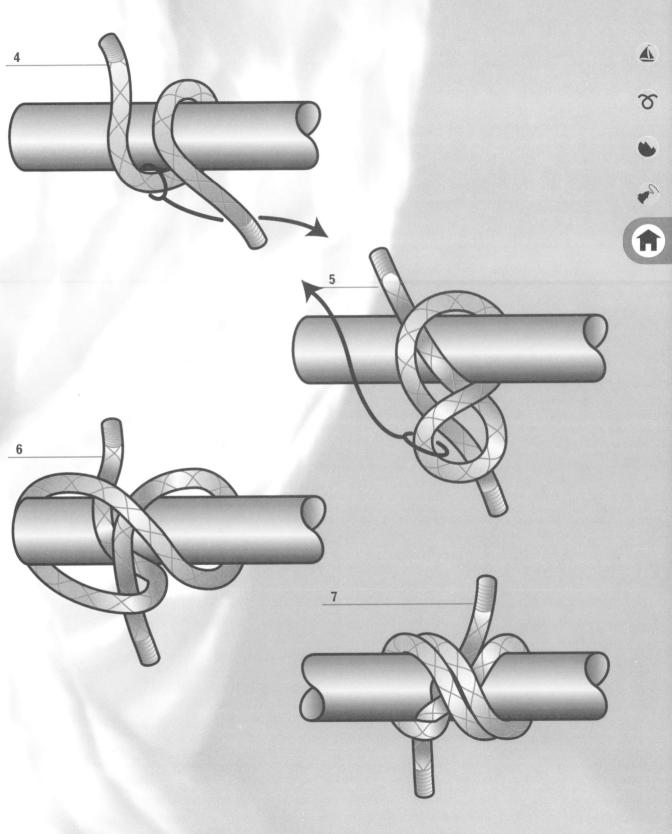

<137>

CONSTRICTOR KNOT (cont'd)

METHOD

One quick way to pick up a knot is to outline an ampersand (figs 8–9); another is to start with an S-shape (figs 10–11). This second variation was suggested by Max Nickols in **Knotting Matters** (April 1996). Single or double constrictors may be done with a draw-loop (figs 12–13).

When tying a constrictor knot around something yielding, such as the neck of a sack, use hard-laid cord that will bite into what it surrounds. On a metal rail or any other hard object, choose soft and stretchy stuff. Either way, the knot will grip like a boa constrictor. (Note that the constrictor knot can leave grooves in materials softer than itself, and should not be used where marks of this kind are not wanted.) To remove the knot, either prise it loose (if you can) or cut it off; sever the overlying diagonal and it will fall neatly away in two halves. Alternatively, leave a draw-loop and it can be easily untied.

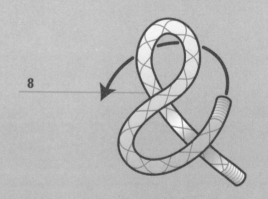

8

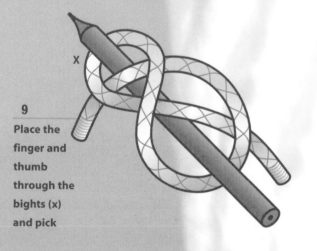

9

Place the finger and thumb through the bights (x) and pick

X

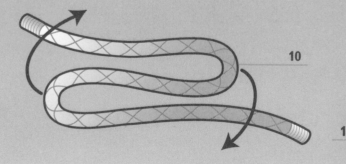

10

11

<138>

HISTORY

Clifford Ashley's genuine claim, made in **The Ashley Book of Knots**, to have discovered this knot has misled many into believing that the constrictor was a relatively new knot in the 1940s when Ashley was writing. Some years earlier, however, a Spaniard, Raphael Gaston, who knew the constrictor as a whip knot used by muleteers and herdsmen in the mountains of Spain, taught it to Finnish Girl Scout leader Martta Ropponen (communicating with her, so the story goes, in Esperanto). She published and illustrated it in 1931. However, the knot had already appeared in a Swedish book published in 1916 (**Om Knutar** by Hjalmar Öhrvall), in which it was called the 'timber knot'. Ashley loyalists point out that, in his book, Ashley tells of tying his constrictor knot over 25 years earlier. Yet in a series of magazine articles on sailors' knots published in 1925, he makes no mention of it. Several members of the International Guild of Knot Tyers – all, it should be emphasized, admirers of Ashley – have researched this knot and established these earlier origins. They are Lester Copestake and Desmond Mandeville (UK), Pieter van de Griend (Faroe Islands) and Sten Johansson (Sweden). Writing in **Knotting Matters** in January 1992, Lester Copestake tells how he spotted an even earlier mention of a gunner's knot, described but unfortunately not illustrated, in his 1890 edition of **The Book of Knots** by Tom Bowling. This knot appears to be identical to the constrictor knot. If this is so, then it seems that the constrictor knot was used in the days of muzzle-loaded big guns to seize the necks of flannel-bag cartridges containing a gunpowder charge. In any case, there is circumstantial but scholarly evidence from Cyrus L. Day, a respected American knot writer, that the constrictor was probably another one of the surgical slings recorded by the Ancient Greek physician Heraklas in the first century AD.

(See **Quipus and Witches' Knots** by Cyrus L. Day.)

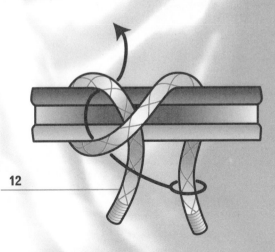

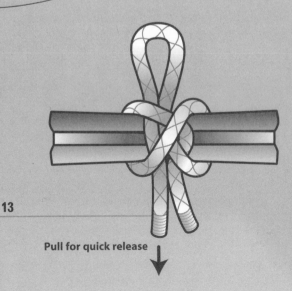

Pull for quick release

<139>

SQUARE KNOT

APPLICATIONS

This is an excellent decorative knot for tying in a scarf around your neck. The bulk of the knot fills the V of an open-neck shirt or blouse, and the ends hang down neatly. The square knot can also secure a dressing-gown cord or other waist-tie belt.

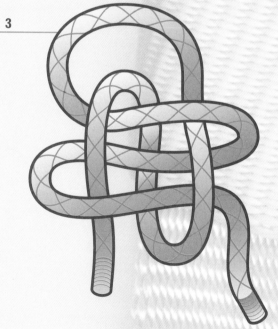

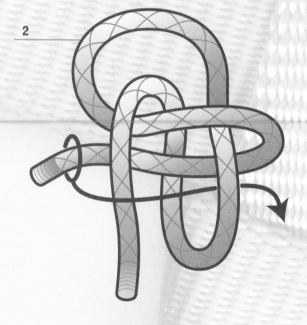

METHOD

Tied beneath the chin, this knot is quick to learn with – or without – a mirror (figs 1–3). The finished knot must be nursed into shape carefully, a bit at a time, by pulling through some slack here and there as necessary. The box-like four-part overlap goes to the front (figs 4-5).

<140>

4
Front view

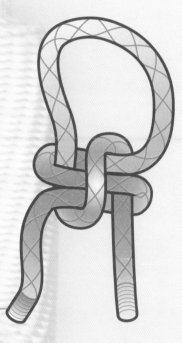

5
Back view

HISTORY

In the US the reef knot is called the square knot, which is presumably why at least one knot book calls the knot illustrated here the 'true square knot'. Another name for it is the rustler's knot. It has also — wrongly, I am advised — been referred to in print as the Chinese good luck knot.

<141>

STRANGLE KNOT

APPLICATIONS

This is a binding knot. (See also constrictor knot, p. 136.)

METHOD

Tie a double overhand knot and slide it onto the object(s) to be bound (figs 1–3). Alternatively, tie it directly and, for a quick release, leave a draw-loop.

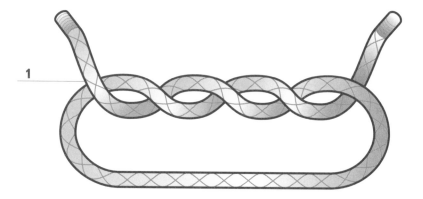

1

2

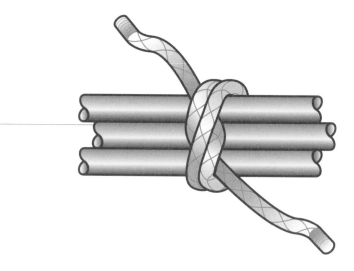

3

HISTORY

Swedish knot expert Hjalmar Öhrvall described this knot in his book **Om Knutar** (1916). He preferred it to the constrictor because its turns lie more snugly together.

<142>

PEDIGREE COW HITCH

APPLICATIONS

This is a quick and simple general-purpose hitch.

METHOD

The common cow hitch (fig. 1) has a working end and a standing part tethered around a rail or post. It is insecure and never to be trusted. To tie this variation, simply tuck and trap the short end through the basic knot (fig. 2). In this way, a previously unreliable knot is made fit for honest work. Leave a draw-loop if you prefer (fig. 3).

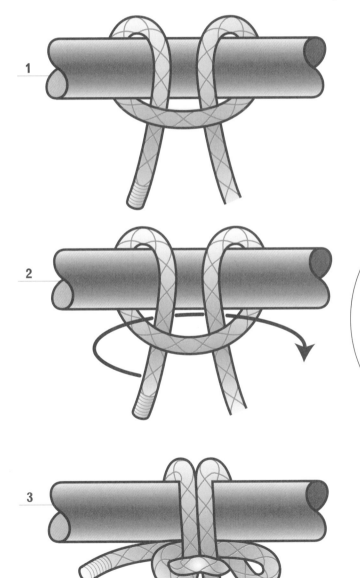

HISTORY

The pedigree cow hitch is formed from a basic cow hitch with the end tucked for extra security. The idea was that of Harry Asher, who published his variation in **The Alternative Knot Book** (1989). It went largely unnoticed by knot enthusiasts until the Girl Guides Association adopted it for level 1 of their Knotter's Badge.

<143>

COW HITCH VARIATION

APPLICATIONS

A stronger version of the common cow hitch, this can be used for all sorts of DIY and craftwork attachments.

METHOD

This knot should be tied directly using a working end (figs 1–3).

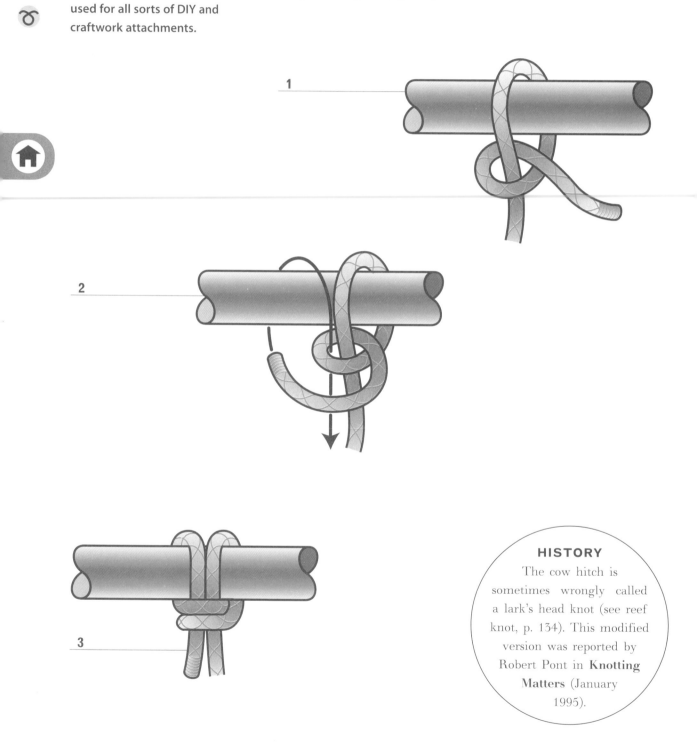

1

2

3

HISTORY

The cow hitch is sometimes wrongly called a lark's head knot (see reef knot, p. 134). This modified version was reported by Robert Pont in **Knotting Matters** (January 1995).

<144>

HALTER HITCH

APPLICATIONS

The halter hitch is a quick-release tether for animals, boats, etc.

METHOD

Tie a slip knot around a ring or rail (fig. 1), dropping the working end through the draw-loop for extra security (figs 2-3). Withdraw the end and tug to release.

HISTORY

This knot was traditionally used wherever working animals were kept.

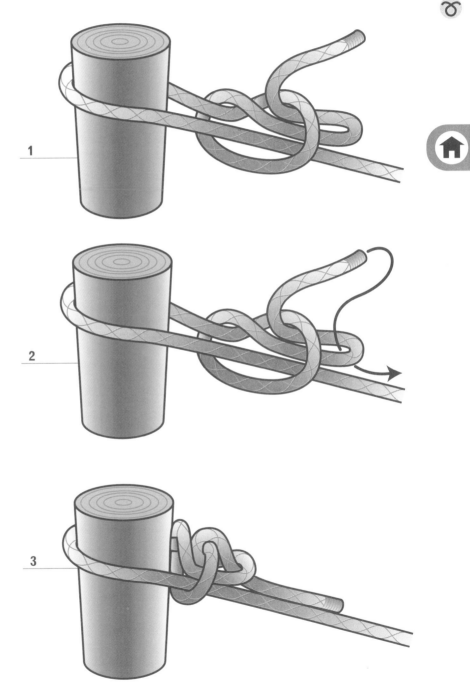

CAT'S PAW

APPLICATIONS

The cat's paw is a strong sling hitch for a heavy load.

1

HISTORY

Known to the Ancient Greeks, this knot was first mentioned by its modern name in David Steel's **Elements and Practice of Rigging and Seamanship** (1794). In 1841 William N. Brady (a boatswain in the US Navy) wrote of the cat's paw in his book **The Naval Apprentice's Kedge Anchor**, and recommended adding two or three twists to it.

2

METHOD

Make sure that the two loops are twisted in opposite directions, one clockwise and the other anti-clockwise (fig. 1). This knot may be pre-tied and passed over the end of a post or rail (figs 2–3) but it must be tied directly onto a ring by means of a number of backward-circling tucks.

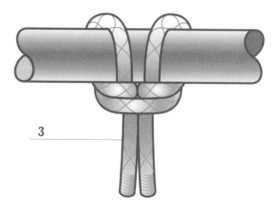

3

<146>

PARCEL TIES

APPLICATIONS

Use this method to secure wrapping paper, large suitcases, cardboard boxes, crates, etc.

HISTORY

Over 50 years ago, before the packaging industry made such manual skills redundant, shopkeepers parcelled and tied goods all day long for customer after customer, their practised fingers forming loops and half-hitches faster than the eye could follow.

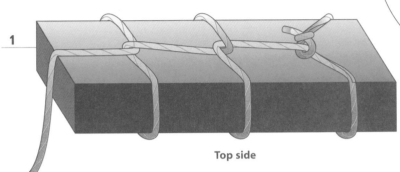

Top side

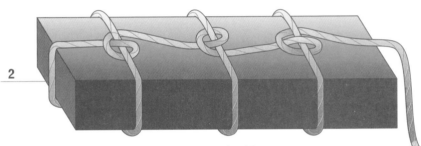

Underside

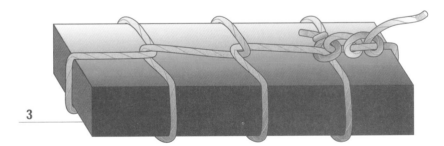

METHOD

Start with a loop in one end of your rope, cord or string – use an overhand loop (see p. 17) or a bowline (perhaps doubled, see p. 36). Pass the other end through the loop. Pull this initial circuit into a shallow V shape. Assemble a series of half-hitches or marline hitches along the length of the parcel (fig. 1, and see pp. 75 and 76). A crossing knot (fig. 2) provides tension at every crossing point on the return journey. Go around the initial V and apply enough tension to flatten it. Finish off with a couple of half-hitches (fig. 3).

<147>

FIREMAN'S CHAIR KNOT

APPLICATIONS

When my two daughters were small I kept a coiled rope upstairs in their first-floor bedroom, as it was too far to drop them to the ground without injury in the event of fire. This knot, with its twin adjustable (and lockable) loops, could have safely lowered them.

METHOD

Tie either a handcuff knot (figs 1–2) or a Tom fool's knot in the bight. Adjust the loops to fit snugly around the chest and knees of the subject. Lock each one with a half-hitch (figs 3–4). The upper long end is used to raise or lower the person, while a second rescuer on the ground holds them clear of any wall, cliff-face, etc. (fig 5).

<148>

HISTORY

Fire Services now use mountain-rescue techniques for upper-floor rescues, but in the past, this knot was used by many firemen. It was also taught by the Scout Association, who started it with a handcuff knot (see p. 66), although the Girl Guides Association and Fire Brigade manuals preferred to start with the Tom fool's knot. Colin Grundy, a professional fire-fighter and member of the International Guild of Knot Tyers, concluded in his **Study of the Chair Knot** (1996) that the handcuff-knot version was better able to retain its shape under repeated loading, due to its greater internal friction. When the load is attached to a **single** loop, the Tom fool's knot allows the loop to be pulled out further, particularly in braided line. However, when **both** loops are loaded, they can be pulled out further by using the handcuff knot. So it seems that either knot would work well enough in a real emergency.

5

<149>

INSTANT KNOT TRICK

APPLICATIONS

In this popular conjuring trick, the knot wizard briefly holds up a doubled cord; then, with a flick of his or her wrist, an overhand knot (see p. 16) appears in it.

METHOD

Use whichever hand comes naturally to you. Double about a metre (3 ft) of cord over one hand (fig. 1). Pick up both ends, ensuring that the one coming from the back of your hand is innermost when you trap them between your fore and middle fingers (fig. 2). Release the outer end, at the same time allowing your wrist to droop (fig. 3). Let the loop of cord fall off your hand. An overhand knot will instantly appear (fig. 4).

HISTORY

Conjuring is an ancient craft and this trick has probably been practised around the world for thousands of years.

1

2
Let arrowed end drop

3
Allow loop to fall off hand

4

<150>

IMPOSSIBLE KNOT TRICK

APPLICATIONS

This is a party or conjuring trick in which the knot wizard challenges his or her audience to tie a knot without letting go of the ends of the cord. They try and fail. The wizard then does it.

METHOD

Using at least 2 metres (6 ft) of cord, and working with your dominant hand, drape a loop over the opposite forearm (fig. 1). Stress to onlookers that the hands are holding both ends throughout the trick. Pass the working hand over-under-over (fig. 2) and return it to its own side once again. Lift the passive hand, and lower the working one. Tell your audience to watch the upper hand, which is where the knot will appear, and concentrate on it yourself, but at the same time quietly change your grip with the lower hand, as shown in fig. 3. The trick is now done and all that remains is to act out the drama of dropping the loop from the back of the upper hand to fall into the impossible overhand knot (fig. 4).

You should not as a rule repeat a knot trick, because this will increase the chance of someone spotting how it is done. However, this trick can be done again ('... even more slowly, so that you can see exactly what I do').

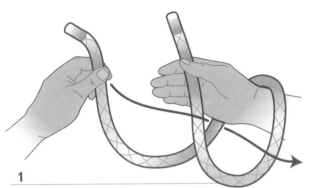

1

Thread this hand over-under-over and return to starting position

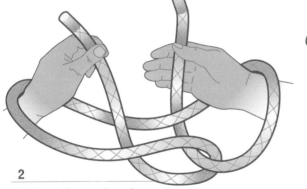

2

The hand changes its grip from here ...

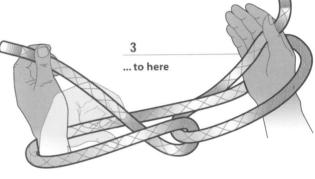

3

... to here

HISTORY

This is, I am sure, another ancient example of the conjuror's art.

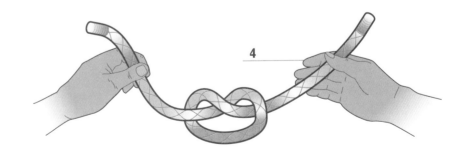

4

<151>

KNOTS GALORE TRICK

APPLICATIONS

This is another sleight of hand. The knot wizard piles a load of seemingly insecure half-hitches over one thumb, on the implausible pretext of demonstrating how he or she won a competition to become the world's greatest knot tyer. The half-hitches are removed and concealed, within a fist, with just one end peeping out. When that end is slowly withdrawn, the cord is found to be knotted at regular intervals.

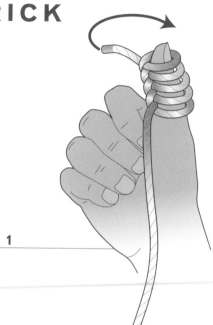

1

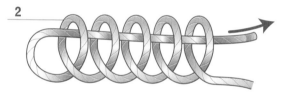

2

METHOD

The half-hitches must all be made the same way (fig. 1). Allow them to spiral around your thumb. Draw them off with the thumb and fingers of your other hand, cunningly ensuring that the working end goes down through all the half-hitches (fig. 2). The resulting bird's nest is then turned upside-down, held gently in a closed fist, and the working end withdrawn slowly and carefully (fig. 3). The overhand knots will form themselves, but some slight manipulation – which need not be concealed – with the fingers and thumb of the enclosing fist is needed to ensure that they emerge in sequence and untangled.

3

HISTORY

This old conjuring trick was also taught to seamen and fire-fighters as a fast way to convert a coil into a full-size climbing rope in an emergency.

<152>

THREADING-THE-NEEDLE TRICK

APPLICATIONS

In this trick, the knot wizard faces his or her audience and, without a word, wraps a thick-ish cord several times around one thumb, leaving a small loop at the end. He or she then makes a couple of vain attempts to thread the other end of the cord through the loop (which is clearly too small for cord plus hand). Then – somehow – the feat is achieved.

HISTORY

Country singer and actor Willy Nelson did this trick to camera in a film. He repeated it once, twice – and the impact was just as good the second and third times.

METHOD

The end of the cord that lies in the fork of the thumb and forefinger is the one you will be threading, so keep it a convenient length, no more than 30 cm (1 ft). With something like 8-mm ($^1/_3$-in) cord, you will fit about four turns onto your thumb before making the loop (fig. 1). This trick will work with a direct loop (fig. 2), but it involves a bit of twiddling to get it right, so reverse the loop (fig. 3) for a trouble-free performance every time. At this stage, keep your fingers straight and together so that your hand masks what will happen next. Pick up the end to be threaded through the loop (fig. 4), make a couple of deliberately unsuccessful attempts, and then simply push the end forward as far as it will go (so that it passes close by the end of the thumb). The trick is done. One turn has disappeared from your thumb (fig. 5) – but it would take a very observant onlooker to spot that.

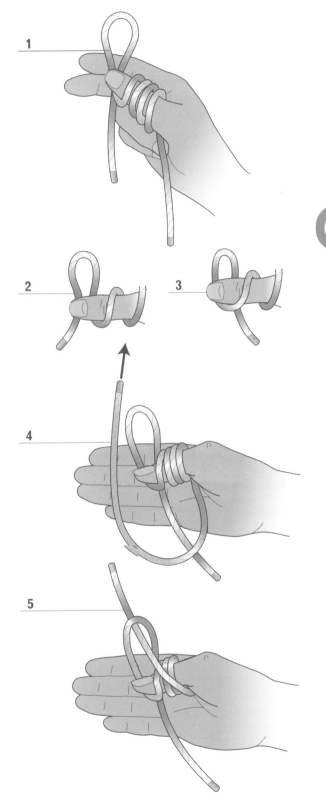

<153>

FINGER-TRAP TRICK

APPLICATIONS

This is another knot trick. The knot wizard, using an endless band of cord, lays down five loops and invites a member of his or her audience either to spear one of the loops with a finger and so trap the cord or chain, or to pass a finger through one of the loops without being caught in it. The victim tries and fails. The helpful wizard reduces the number of loops to four, then three, two and one, but to no avail. If the victim does not succeed in trapping the loop, then he is trapped by it instead. He cannot win.

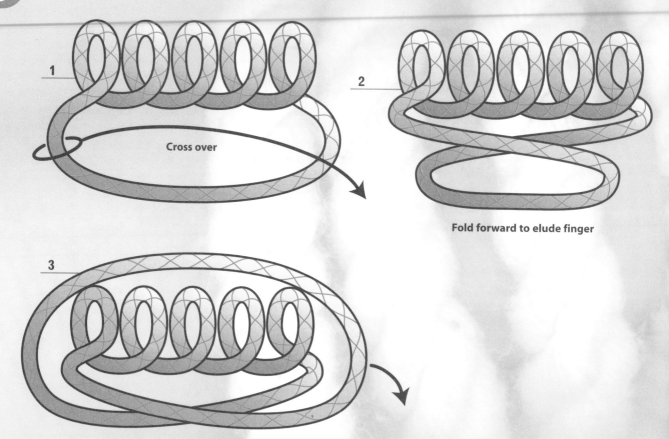

1

Cross over

2

Fold forward to elude finger

3

Pull away from any point on the surrounding loop

<154>

METHOD

Use about 2 metres (6 ft) of 6-mm (^{1}/$_4$-in) flexible cord with the ends tied together, or sealed, to form an endless band. A flexible ornamental chain is even better. Once a victim has nominated 'trap' or 'elude', the rest of the cord loop is crossed over and folded forward to enclose the finger loops and achieve the opposite effect. Figs 1-3 show how to elude the finger,

and figs 4-5 how to trap it. To onlookers, the layout seems identical. Pull the cord away from anywhere you like – you can even allow the participants to nominate a point. Harmless betting for nominal stakes enhances the fun.

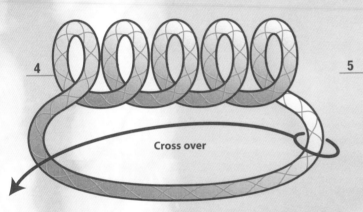

4

Cross over

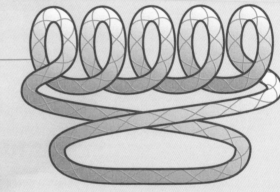

5

Fold forward to trap finger

6

Pull away from any point on the surrounding loop

HISTORY

This is a very old confidence trick, which street and fairground performers have long used to separate the unwary from their money.

<155>

GLOSSARY

Abseil	To descend an anchored climbing rope in a controlled way (also known as rappelling)
Anchor	An attachment for securing vessels on sea or river bed; a safety device for climbers (see **Belay**)
Barrel knot	See **Blood knot**
Belay	To secure or anchor a climbing position with ropes and fixings
Bend	The generic name for the many knots that join two separate ropes
Bight	An acute bend or partial loop in a rope
Blood knot	Any one of a group of strong and secure barrel-shaped knots, with characteristic wrapping turns, particularly favoured by anglers and climbers
Breaking strength	The manufacturer's calculation of the load that will cause a rope to fail, taking no account of any weakening factors (see **Safe working load**)
Cable	A large rope laid up left-handed (i.e., S-laid) from three hawser-laid ropes
Capsize	(Of knots) To become deformed due to incorrect tying or misuse, or in untying
Cord	Line under 25-mm (1-in) in circumference or approximately 10-mm ($^1/_2$-in) in diameter (see **Small stuff**)
Core	The filler (or heart) in the centre of rope and cordage, made from fibres or monofilaments
Dog	To secure the working end of a rope by wrapping it several times around its own standing part, or another rope
Efficiency	The strength of any knot, as a percentage of the breaking strength of the rope or cordage in which it is tied
Elbow	Two crossing points created close together by a bight
End	The working end or free end of a rope or cordage (see **Standing end**)
Eye	A loop commonly in the end of a line
Fibre	The smallest element in vegetable-rope construction, twisted to create yarns (see **Staple**)
Filament	See **Monofilament**
Fray	Deliberate or accidental unlaying of a rope, causing it to be teased out into its component strands and yarns
Hard eye	An eye reinforced with a metal or plastic thimble
Hard laid	(Of rope and cordage) Highly tensioned during manufacture
Hawser	Any three-stranded rope over 25-mm (1-in) in circumference or 10-mm ($^1/_2$-in) in diameter.
Heart	See **Core**
Hitch	The generic name for any knot used to attach a line to a ring, rail or post (or to another line, or even to itself)
Karabiner	A D-shaped or pear-shaped metal snap-ring, with a pivoting gate that can be securely closed; used by climbers
Knot	The general name for all rope and cordage entanglements, but specifically one tied in the end of a line, or with both ends of the same line, or in small stuff
Lanyard	A short length of cord used to lash or secure an item of equipment
Lay	The direction in which rope strands and yarns spiral (i.e., right- or left-handed)
Lead	(Say 'leed') The direction taken by cordage around or through an object or knot
Leader	A short length of gut, monofilament, braid or wire attaching a fishing hook to a line
Line	Any rope with a particular function; e.g., a tow line, clothes-line or mooring line
Loop	A bight with a crossing point
Make fast	To secure a line to an anchorage or belay

<156>

Messenger	A light line used to pull a heavier working rope or cable into position
Middle	To double a rope or cord prior to use
Monofilament	Long synthetic thread; the smallest element of man-made ropes
Natural fibre	Raw material used in vegetable-rope construction
Nip	The point within a knot where friction is concentrated
Noose	A sliding loop
Rappel	See **Abseil**
Reef	To roll up (or fold and tie) sails, reducing their area in strong wind
Reeve	To thread the end of a rope through a pulley block, etc.
Rope	Any line over 25-mm (1-in) in circumference or about 10-mm ($^1/_2$-in) in diameter; larger than cord
Round turn	In which a working end completely encircles a ring, rail, post or another line, and is then brought alongside its own standing part
S-laid	(Of rope) Left-handed
Safe working load	The estimated load a rope may safely withstand, taking into account its age, condition and usage; it may be as little as one-sixth of the quoted breaking strength (see **Breaking strength**)
Security	A knot's integral ability to withstand intermittent tugs, shaking, etc.
Sling	A knotted or spliced endless band or strop
Small stuff	A casual and imprecise term for any cordage (as opposed to rope)
Soft laid	(Of rope and cordage) Flexible due to the absence of tension in manufacture
Standing end	The opposite end of a line from the working end
Standing part	That part of rope and cordage between the working and standing ends
Staple	Graded fibres, of limited length due to their vegetable origins
Strand	The main element of rope, made in its turn from contra-twisted yarns
Strength	A knot's integral ability to withstand a load
String	Domestic-quality small cord or twine
Strop	See **Sling**
Synthetic rope	Rope and cordage made from monofilaments
Tag end	An angling term for the working end of a line
Thimble	A metal or plastic reinforcement for seized or spliced eyes; used in sailing
Thread	Fine line
Turn	A 360-degree wrap around a ring, rail, post or rope
Whipping	A method of binding a rope's end to prevent fraying
Working end	The end of rope or cord that is available for use
Yarn	The basic element of rope strands, itself made of fibres or monofilaments
Z-laid	(Of rope) Right-handed

<157>

BIBLIOGRAPHY

The content of this book has been influenced by the following writers, living and dead, whose original publications I gratefully acknowledge. I have also drawn on comprehensive unpublished correspondence (1978 to the present) from *Robert Chisnall on the subject of climbers' knots.

PRIMARY SOURCES

*Asher, Harry, **The Alternative Knot Book**,
    Nautical Books/A. & C. Black (1989)
Ashley, Clifford W., **The Ashley Book of Knots**,
    Doubleday, Doran & Co. (1944)/Faber & Faber (1947)
Bailey, Hazel, **Knotting for Guides**, Girl Guides Association (1987)
Barnes, Stanley, **Anglers' Knots in Gut and Nylon**, Cornish Brothers (1948)
*Blandford, Percy W., **Practical Knots and Ropework**, Tab Books (1980)
Bowling, Tom, **The Book of Knots**, Hardwicke & Bogue (1876)
British Army, **Instruction in Military Engineering** (1887)
British Mountaineering Council, **Knots booklet** (undated)
Clements, Rex, **A Gypsy of the Horn** (1924)
Day, Cyrus L., **Quipus and Witches' Knots**, University of Kansas (1967)
Gerber, Ham, **Making Discoveries in Knots**,
    Binford & Mort Publishing (1990)
Girl Guides Association, **Knots for Everybody** (1980)
Grant, Bruce, **Encyclopedia of Rawhide and Leather Braiding**,
    Cornell Maritime Press (1972)
Hunter, W.A., **Fisherman's Knots and Wrinkles**, A. & C. Black (1927)
International Guild of Knot Tyers, **Knotting Matters**
    (quarterly journal/October 1982 to date)
Jacobson, Cliff, **Knots for the Outdoors**, ICS Books (1990)
*Jones, Colin, **The Fender Book**, self-published (1996)
Kreh, Lefty, and Sosin, Mark, **Practical Fishing and Boating Knots**,
    A. & C. Black (1975)
Lever, Darcy, **Sheet Anchor**, London (1808)
Luebben, Craig, **Knots for Climbers**, Chockstone Press (1993)
Maclean, William P., **Modern Marlinspike Seamanship**,
    David & Charles (1982)
March, Bill, **Modern Rope Techniques in Mountaineering**,
    Cicerone Press (1976)
*Merry, Barbara, **The Splicing Handbook**,
    International Marine Publishing Co. (1987)
Ontario Rock Climbing Association, **Rock Climbing Safety Manual** (1984)
Owen, Peter, **The Book of Outdoor Knots**, Lyons & Burford (1993)
Owen, Peter, **Identifying Knots**, Quintet Publishing (1996)
*Rosenow, Frank, **Seagoing Knots**, W.W. Norton & Co. (1990)
Smith, Hervey Garrett, **The Arts of the Sailor**,
    D. Van Nostrand Company (1953)
Smith, Hervey Garrett, **The Marlinespike Sailor**, David & Charles (1972)
Smith, Phil D., **Knots for Mountaineering**, self-published (1975)
Sweet, John, **Scout Pioneering**, The Scout Association (1974)
Tarbuck, Ken, **Nylon Rope and Climbing Safety**,
    British Ropes Ltd (undated)
*Toss, Brion, **The Rigger's Apprentice**,
    International Marine Publishing Co. (1984)
*Toss, Brion, **Knots**, Hearst Marine Books (1990)
*Toss, Brion, **The Rigger's Locker**, International Marine/Tab Books (1992)
*Trower, Nola, **Knots and Ropework**,
    Helmsman Books/The Crowood Press (1992)
*Turner, J.C., and *van de Griend, P. (editors), **History and Science of Knots**,
    World Scientific Publishing Co. (1996)
*Warner, Charles, **A Fresh Approach to Knotting and Ropework**,
    self-published (1992)
Wheelock, Walt, **Ropes, Knots and Slings for Climbers**,
    La Siesta Press (1967)
* IGKT members

SECONDARY SOURCES (referred to in the above publications)

Brady, William N., **The Naval Apprentice's Kedge Anchor**, New York (1841)
Diderot, Denis, **Encyclopédie**, Paris (1762)
Falconer, William, **An Universal Dictionary of the Marine**, London (1769)
Lescallier, M., **Vocabulaires des Termes de Marine**, London (1783)
Little, E.N., **Log Book Notes**, (1889)
Manwayring, Sir Henry, **The Sea-man's Dictionary** (1644)
Öhrvall, Hjalmar, **Om Knutar**, Stockholm (1916)
Riesenberg, Felix, **Seamanship for the Merchant Service**, New York (1922)
Röding, Johann, **Allgemeines Wörterbuch der Marine**, Hamburg (1795)
Steel, David, **Elements and Practice of Rigging and Seamanship**,
    London (1794)
Walton, Isaak, **The Compleat Angler**, London (1653)

THE INTERNATIONAL GUILD OF KNOT TYERS

The International Guild of Knot Tyers was founded by 27 individuals in April 1982 and now has a membership of nearly 1,000 in countries from Australia to Zimbabwe. The IGKT is a registered UK educational charity and anyone interested in knots may join.

Guild members are a friendly crowd, novice and expert alike, brought together by their common pursuit of knot tying. Members within travelling distance may enjoy two major weekend meetings held in England each year, with talks, demonstrations and tuition, where tools, cordage and books (both new and second-hand) are also bought and sold or swapped. In areas where many Guild members live, national or regional branches have been formed. These arrange more frequent gatherings and activity programmes.

The thinly scattered worldwide IGKT membership keeps in touch via a members' handbook and the quarterly magazine, **Knotting Matters**, which is full of informed articles, expert tips, letters, editorial comment, news and views about everything imaginable on the knot-tying scene. The Guild also sells its own instructional publications, postcards and other knotting supplies by mail order.

A few Guild members trade commercially in specialized rope and cordage, tools, accessories and books (new, second-hand and rare) unobtainable elsewhere. They also sell off-the-peg and bespoke (made to order) knot display boards and other ropework items – practical or decorative – from fenders to bellropes. Their expert advice is freely available to customers.

For more details and an application form contact:

Nigel Harding (IGKT Hon. Secretary)
3 Walnut Tree Meadow
Stonham Aspal
Stowmarket
Suffolk IP14 6DF
England

Tel: (01449) 711 121

<158>

INDEX

<159>

<160>